LEADERSHIP THE GANDHI WAY

Virender Kapoor is a thinker, an educationist and an inspirational guru. An alumnus of IIT Bombay and the former director of a prestigious management institute under the Symbiosis umbrella, he is currently the founder-director, president and chief mentor of Management Institute for Leadership and Excellence (MILE), Pune. His books on emotional intelligence, leadership and self-help have been translated into several regional and foreign languages. To know more about him, log on to www.virenderkapoor.com or mail him at virenderkapoor21@yahoo.com

LEADERSHIP THE GANDHI WAY

VIRENDER KAPOOR

Published by
Rupa Publications India Pvt. Ltd 2014
7/16, Ansari Road, Daryaganj
New Delhi 110002

Sales centres:
Allahabad Bengaluru Chennai
Hyderabad Jaipur Kathmandu
Kolkata Mumbai

Copyright © Virender Kapoor 2014

All rights reserved.

No part of this publication may be reproduced, transmitted, or stored in a retrieval system, in any form or by any means, electronic, mechanical, photocopying, recording or otherwise, without the prior permission of the publisher.

ISBN: 978-81-291-3457-8

First impression 2014

10 9 8 7 6 5 4 3 2 1

The moral right of the author has been asserted.

Typeset in Adobe Garamond by SÜRYA, New Delhi
Printed at: Gopsons Papers Ltd., Noida

This book is sold subject to the condition that it shall not, by way of trade or otherwise, be lent, resold, hired out, or otherwise circulated, without the publisher's prior consent, in any form of binding or cover other than that in which it is published.

CONTENTS

PREFACE	vii
PRELUDE *Struggle of a Saint*	xi
1. SATYAGRAHA *The Audacity of Truth*	1
2. ABSOLUTE RIGOROUS INTEGRITY *To Grow from Truth to Truth*	7
3. ART OF COMMUNICATION *How to Share Your Goals with People*	14
4. THE GANDHIAN PHILOSOPHY *Redefining Non-violence as a Way of Life*	24
5. THOUGHT LEADERS NEED AN EXTERNAL COMPASS *People, Personalities and Philosophies*	36
6. FROM 'KAUN' TO ICON *360-degree Brand Building, the Gandhi Way*	44

7. LEADING FROM THE FRONT 57
   The Mahatma, a Brilliant Organizer

8. SELF-DISCIPLINE AND SELF-CONDUCT 69
   Saint and Soldier

9. GANDHI'S CHARISMA 82
   Something that Money Can't Buy

10. COLLABORATIVE SUCCESS 89
    Role of a Spouse in a Leader's Life

11. SPIRITUALIZATION OF POLITICS 100
    Benevolent Leadership, a Paradigm Shift

12. SIMPLIFY YOUR LIFE 112
    Minimalistic Living

PREFACE

'Generations to come, it may well be, will scarcely believe that such a man as this one ever in flesh and blood walked upon this Earth.'
—Albert Einstein on Mahatma Gandhi

This is not a biography of Mohandas K. Gandhi. Rather, it is a book about leadership, and the lessons that can be derived from Gandhi's life and death. *Leadership: The Gandhi Way* is a unique take on the Mahatma who, even more than sixty years after his death, continues to be an inspiration not only in India but across the world. His is a legacy that endures; his message will never go stale.

What was it about Gandhi that made him a timeless icon? Was he born a Mahatma (literally, 'a great soul') or was he transformed into one? How could a man like him, frail-looking, nondescript, a lawyer by education, lead a nation of 30 million people and make them think the way he himself did? How could one man be a messiah for the poor and the destitute, and a guiding light for the intelligentsia and the elite at the same time? With hardly any material means at his command he reached out to people not only in his own country but also to a few thousand Indians in a far-off continent in South Africa. He was a saint, a soldier in action and a leader of millions of his countrymen—a leader without authority. This book will answer three pertinent questions: What can we learn from Mahatma Gandhi as far as leadership is concerned? Was there anything new about his style of leadership? And can we put those lessons into good use, almost a century after Gandhi lived?

Most Indians learn about Mahatma Gandhi in school. Many, though, would miss out on the essential lessons of his life and success, as well as his work style. Most books written about this great soul are very detailed and highly philosophical, and can often be intimidating because of their sheer volume. Many would thus find the available material to be uninteresting and preachy.

My endeavour was to write a book that is easy to read, yet covers the entire canvas. The focus is on leadership. I aim to tell the readers and the leaders of this century that, indeed, you can learn from Gandhi and lead like him. This book will bring Mahatma Gandhi closer to many Indians who have never read about him in detail.

The challenge was threefold:

- To put across the concept briefly and yet convey what matters most.
- To reach out to the uninitiated by keeping it simple.
- To offer practical lessons so that a reader not only connects with the message but is also able to apply most of the leadership traits of this great man.

I address all three points. Having written several books on leadership, motivation, emotional intelligence, and work–life balance in the past, this was a refreshing challenge. I could draw upon my past experience to bring out the best of Gandhi for readers who want to make better leaders of themselves.

PREFACE

While writing this book I was amazed to discov[er]
relevant Gandhi's style of leadership remains in today's
The key is to adapt to—rather than adopt—his philoso[phy]
action and it will work for sure.

PRELUDE

Struggle of a Saint

Born on 2 October 1869 at Porbandar, Gujarat, Mohandas Karamchand Gandhi was not an extraordinary student in his schooldays. He was obedient and soft-spoken. He got married at the age of thirteen to Kasturba, who was a year older than him.

In 1888, at the age of eighteen, he left India without his wife and newborn baby to study law in London. As a student he emulated the British by wearing expensive clothes to look like a gentleman. Again, as a student in England, he did not perform in any spectacular manner.

He returned to India in 1891 and tried to practise law, but did not succeed. He was offered a job as a lawyer in South Africa and sailed for this foreign land at the age of twenty-three. While in South Africa he realized that the British treated the natives and Indians settled there very badly. He himself was thrown out of a first-class train compartment, even though he carried a valid ticket, only on account of his being an Indian. He decided to fight back not only for his own dignity but also for the rest of the Indians living there.

For more than a decade he became the messiah of the Indians in South Africa; it was his learning ground. At the young age of twenty-five he formed the Natal Indian Congress (NIC) for his activism. Soon, many joined him and with the help of his supporters he established two ashrams: one known as Tolstoy Farm on 1,100 acres of land, and the other, the Phoenix settlement, which was over 100 acres. Gandhi came up with the idea of non-violence and coined the word 'Satyagraha', which means 'polite insistence'. Satyagrahis were trained in these ashrams where the mantra was simple living and high thinking. In his twenty years in South Africa, he led many campaigns against apartheid, went on fasts and was jailed several times. He was a public figure who gradually became famous across the world.

Gandhi returned to India in 1901 and travelled several times between South Africa and India. Eventually he left South Africa in 1914 and established his ashram at Kochrab near Ahmedabad in 1915. For the next few years he led Satyagraha-based campaigns for peasants and mill workers. He established the Sabarmati Ashram in 1917, which later became the epicentre for the Indian freedom movement. By 1918–19 Gandhi took the British head-on and organized a nationwide 'hartal' or strike against the Rowlatt Act, which was a harsh law that defined and punished the crime of sedition.

By 1921 Gandhi was in full control of the Indian freedom movement. By now he had travelled across the country to be with the people and feel their pulse. He literally shed his clothes and wore only a loincloth. Mass civil disobedience was started against the British by him, which was later abandoned as violence broke out at Chauri Chaura near Gorakhpur due to the over-enthusiasm of Satyagrahis. He realized that India was yet not ready for a full-fledged Satyagraha andolan. He was sentenced to a jail term of six years in Yerwada jail in Pune, for charges of sedition. He was released in 1924.

Thereafter he was made the president of the Indian National Congress. Under his leadership the Congress passed a resolution in 1928 calling for the country's complete independence within one year.

The British did not heed this request. In 1930 Gandhi, along with some seventy-eight Satyagrahis, went on a 240-mile-long march from Sabarmati Ashram to Dandi and broke the colonial 'Salt Law' by making salt from sea water. It was a peaceful, legendary protest against the salt tax that Gandhi believed was unjust.

He was again imprisoned in 1932, where he began his fast unto death against the British for giving a separate electorate to untouchables. This ended with the Poona Pact signed by Dr Babasaheb Ambedkar. Gandhi was totally against untouchability and from the very beginning of his activitism he did everything in his power to help erase it.

In 1942 under Gandhi's leadership, the Congress started the 'Quit India' movement, which was a nationwide Satyagraha campaign to oust the British from Indian soil. Gandhi was arrested and imprisoned at the Aga Khan Palace in Pune along with his wife Kasturba and some other Congress leaders. He was released in 1944 due to poor health. Kasturba died the same year.

During the period between 1945 and 1947, Gandhi's main preoccupation was to quell the communal tension between the country's Hindus and Muslims. He was also discussing the modalities of India's freedom with the British, especially with Lord Mountbatten.

On 15 August 1947 India acquired its independence and got partitioned into two nations: India and Pakistan. Intense violence and riots broke out in many parts of the country. Gandhi went on a fast to stop the violence. Thousands of Hindus and Muslims perished in the catastrophe of a very large magnitude.

After the country acquired independence, the top priority of the government was to rehabilitate those who had suffered the wrath of Partition. Gandhi was totally involved in stopping the riots and communal tensions.

On 30 January 1948, on a wintry evening, he was assassinated at Birla House in Delhi by Nathuram Godse.

1

SATYAGRAHA

The Audacity of Truth

*'Non-violence is the first article of my faith.
It is also the last article of my creed.'*
—Mahatma Gandhi

Birth of a Concept

Right from the beginning, Mahatma Gandhi embarked upon non-violence to protest against the British Raj. He knew that any other method which resorted to violence was bound to fail as the British were very strong not only militarily but in every other respect. What Gandhi initiated was a new way of making demands from the establishment, which would later become his biggest weapon and the founding principle of his political philosophy for the freedom struggle. Gandhi's resistance movement ushered in a new era of civilian—and civilized—protests, which inspired many political leaders across the world.

Origin of a New Word: 'Satyagraha'

Mahatma Gandhi, during his struggle against the oppressive British rule in South Africa, initially called his non-violent movement 'passive resistance'. But he wanted a more apt term in the vernacular that would highlight the spirit of his movement, which was based on moral courage, strength and truth. A competition for suggesting names was held in *Indian Opinion*, a local newspaper, and the best entry was for 'sadagraha' (a polite insistence) which was then modified to 'Satyagraha' by Gandhi. 'Satyagraha' was a combination of 'satya', meaning the truth, and 'agraha' meaning insistence. He called it the 'soul force' which was to be a weapon of the strong and insisted upon truth and non-violence in all circumstances.

Basis of Gandhi's Philosophy of Satyagraha

This was a well-thought-out political strategy and was based on the idea of truth which was time-tested by religions like Jainism and Buddhism and also talked about in the Upanishads. 'Ahinsa' or non-violence was at the core of these religious beliefs. Viewed at a personal level, it meant hard work and commitment to truth.

The basic idea of Satyagraha is to make the opponent see reason and realize the evil that the opponent is indulging in. By repeatedly pleading using peaceful means, it makes him realize the injustice being done to others. When you are protesting peacefully, there is little chance of any opponent resorting to violence. After all, your opponent also has a heart and a conscience.

Methodology

Protests were undertaken as peaceful marches, with no foul language, nor use of physical force. It was civil disobedience or 'civilized disobedience' or 'gentlemanly disobedience'. Ultimately the people participating in such protests prepared themselves for arrest. It later manifested as hartals and boycotts, bringing life to a standstill. Gandhi started this with the idea of changing the heart of the opponent. It also changed the heart of all the Indians witnessing the movement. As a result, an increasing number of people joined the civil disobedience movement. Since it did not require physical force, lakhs of people participated, including women and children. Such peaceful protests also brought about a change of heart for some Britishers, who indirectly started speaking for the freedom fighters. Gradually, reports and photographs of this extraordinary protest started appearing in the press across the world. This triggered a worldwide support for the Indian freedom movement, and world opinion turned in favour of Gandhi, enough to put pressure on the British government to free India.

Commitment and Discipline

Gandhi expected self-discipline from every Satyagrahi. Satyagraha was based on sacrifice, simplicity and renunciation. Every Satyagrahi was to shun untouchability and be a supporter of secularism. Gandhi realized that for the movement to succeed, it had to be pan-religious as Hindus, Muslims, Sikhs and Christians were in sizeable numbers. Gandhi expected people to work for their own food, and embrace khadi, or homespun cloth, that represented self-reliance and simplicity.

Selling the Concept to the People

On the face of it, the concept of Satyagraha appeared impractical to most and strange to others. Nobody, perhaps not even Gandhi himself realized the potency of this simple weapon at that point of time. It was indeed a unique experiment.

Satyagraha was difficult to implement, based as it was on the powers of truth, patience, and discipline. The basic problem was that protestors, even huge crowds of them, were supposed to remain calm in the face of instigation by the British. This was very difficult to maintain all the time and at different locations. Obviously, Gandhi could not be present at every location at all times to calm the protestors.

On 5 February 1922, a crowd of almost 3,000 protestors turned violent while carrying out a peace march at Chauri Chaura in Gorakhpur district. This led to the police opening fire and the protestors retaliating by burning the police station. A number of protestors and policemen were killed in the mayhem. Gandhi had to call off the non-cooperation movement at the national level following this incident. Many protestors were arrested and several sentenced to death following conviction in a trial. Gandhi realized that Indians were not yet fully trained for exercising such restraint in the face of the British, who were always ready to demonstrate their power and hence instigate or incite the crowd to retaliate violently.

Despite these difficulties and initial hurdles, non-violence and Satyagraha went on to become very effective tools for the Gandhian movement. It was later adopted very successfully by Nelson Mandela and Martin Luther King to protest against racial discrimination in their respective countries.

Satyagraha in Business Leadership

Satyagraha is all about human will, faith in a cause and truth. Several successful examples of a leadership strategy similar to Satyagraha can be found in the business world. Jim Collins, in his book, *Good to Great* (Random House, 2006), says, 'You must maintain unwavering faith that you can and will prevail in the end, regardless of difficulties.' At the same time, he says, you should have the discipline to face reality, however brutal it may be. The companies described in the book grew from being merely 'good' to becoming 'great' by the sheer will and characteristic humility of their top leaders, virtues that percolated all the way down through the employees' ranks. In corporate parlance, such type of leader is sometimes referred to as the 'selfless executive' or 'servant leader', or 'leader without a title.' There is a striking similarity between what Gandhi practised and what Jim Collins observed in many great corporate leaders. One lesson that all of them showed by example is that one can achieve almost anything with a clear goal, tremendous resolve, truth and honesty of purpose.

There are a number of contemporary business leaders who follow this path, including Narayana Murthy of India's Infosys; Bill Gates at Microsoft in the US; the deceased Steve Jobs at Apple; and the Tatas' nurturing a value-based Tata Group in India.

At the individual level, too, a similar resolve based on willpower and a spirit of 'I can and I will' in every adverse situation can make a person highly successful. One has to be true to one's own resolve and move towards spiritual discipline to achieve goals.

'I regard myself as a soldier, though a soldier of peace.'
—M.K. Gandhi

LEADERSHIP LESSONS FROM A SAINT WITHOUT AUTHORITY

1. Gandhi understood that the British, who were his opponents, were very strong and any method of protest involving violence would be easily crushed and hence he chose non-violence as a weapon. Leaders must therefore do a SWOT analysis of a situation and only then formulate a strategy.
2. Leaders, while dealing with people, must understand the power of emotional appeal. Gandhi was able to relate nationalism with self-esteem very effectively, thus connecting with the hearts of Indians of all faiths.
3. A leader should know how far is too far. After the Chauri Chaura incident Gandhi demonstrated his ability to judge a situation by calling off the non-cooperation movement.
4. With firm resolve, honesty of purpose and personal integrity, a leader can achieve almost anything.

2

ABSOLUTE RIGOROUS INTEGRITY

To Grow from Truth to Truth

'Real integrity is doing the right thing, knowing that nobody's going to know whether you did it or not.'
—Oprah Winfrey, US television host

Living by Your Own Conscience

One can live one's life with integrity by adhering to a moral code in a steadfast manner. This moral code is defined largely by our own conscience and within the context of the society we live in. Use of right action for the right cause or right reason is essential for understanding the applicability of integrity. For instance, a knife when used by a surgeon to save a life is an act which is in the spirit of integrity; but a knife used by a thief to kill someone is not. Using a plastic bucket to store water is correct but throwing broken old plastic buckets into the sea for disposal is not. For the common man, integrity represents uncorrupted virtue and a sense of goodness. Mahatma Gandhi's sense of integrity was based on his famous quote, 'To believe in something and not to live it is dishonest.'

Integrity is also about one's intentions. If your intentions are good then you are honest and upright, but if your intention is bad then you are not.

Two young monks were travelling on a muddy track near a village. It started raining heavily and the track became very slushy. The two saw a beautiful young girl in a silk dress, who was unable to walk and reach the village temple. The older one took the initiative and lifted the girl in his arms, carrying her safely to the temple. Next day the younger monk said, 'You know we monks are not supposed to touch women, especially young and beautiful ones. Why did you do that?' The older one replied, 'I left the girl there yesterday. Are you still carrying her?' Therefore, looking at it in another way: 'Integrity is all in the mind.'

Always by Example

Mahatma Gandhi practised what he preached and I feel this is one of the basic tenets of integrity. There is a famous story about Gandhi which demonstrates this quality in him. It goes like this:

There was a boy who was very fond of eating sweets. His mother was concerned with this bad habit and knew that it would harm his health in the long run. She explained this to him several times but no amount of scolding helped.

His mother knew that for her son, Gandhi was like a god. She decided to take him to the Mahatma. Upon reaching his ashram she told Gandhi, 'Bapu, my son eats too many sweets and too much sugar, which is bad for his health. Can you please advise him to stop eating sweets?' Gandhi looked at her with concern and said, 'Please go now, and bring him back after a month.' The woman got very upset and was surprised by Gandhi's answer.

But, as told, she brought her son back to Gandhi after a month. He told the boy, 'You should stop eating so much sugar. It is bad for your health.' The boy's mother asked Bapu, 'But why didn't you tell him to quit sugar a month back?' Bapu replied, 'Because a month back, I myself was eating a lot of sugar. How could I tell him not to?'

This is a very important lesson at the personal level. When business leaders or people in power preach about something but do the opposite, they lose their credibility.

Building Trust

It came as a surprise to many that Gandhi was able to influence such large numbers of people from different segments of society. In fact, Gandhi won the people's trust because he lived by his word and demonstrated integrity in every aspect of his life. He did this very consciously so that his ideology was embraced by all those who wanted to join hands with him for his mission.

Mahatma Gandhi never lost a chance to demonstrate that he lived according to his principles. When he was in South Africa, the British had to fight two wars: one was the war against the Boer community, and the other was known as the Zulu war. Gandhi felt that Indians in South Africa should serve the British Empire by joining their reserve army. This was much before he started his protest against the British for racial discrimination. He himself volunteered to work in the Indian Ambulance Corps as a stretcher bearer. He even received awards for this. However, once he started protesting against the British rule in South Africa, he felt he could no longer retain those awards on moral grounds. Since the context changed, his decision changed, and he wrote a letter to the viceroy returning the Kaiser-i-Hind gold medal and the Zulu as well as Boer war medals. No wonder Gandhi said that he was moving from truth to truth.

Sartorial Integrity

'Sartorial' refers to the way one dresses up. For instance, lawyers wear a black coat and a white shirt when at court, and formal conferences have a defined dress code. Mahatma Gandhi realized that a lot could be conveyed about your intentions, your honesty and the values you stand for by the way you dress up.

When he went to Britain to study law, he was very impressed by the way the British dressed. He was all for imitating them and hence bought himself expensive suits, neck ties, shirts and hats. He was so enamoured by the British social norms that he decided to write a small handbook called 'Guide to London', meant for Indian students coming to England. He did not want to be a misfit in the English society and made genuine efforts to be dressed like a gentleman all the time.

When he reached South Africa, he landed at Durban as a well-dressed young advocate. He was under the impression that the English dress code would give him social respectability. But he soon realized that Indians were looked down upon by the British and there was deep prejudice against them. Regardless of what they wore, Indians were treated very shabbily in public places in South Africa, such as restaurants and trains. In England, Gandhi had not experienced such discrimination. He felt that even well-to-do Indians were not treated with respect by the British and the poor were treated very badly. Gandhi spent more than a decade in South Africa and during this period he gradually shunned the life of luxury and moved towards what he called 'simplicity and self reliance'. He started washing his own clothes and cutting his own hair. His clothes were not as well-starched as before and therefore his other lawyer friends made fun of him. This only made him stronger; no amount of ridicule could pull him down. He realized at this time the importance of personal integrity over social acceptance. He now got more inclined to do social work. He founded the Phoenix settlement in 1904, which was an experiment in communal living, ethical behaviour, education and simplicity. His friend, a German named Hermann Kallenbach, gifted him 1,100 acres of farmland where Gandhi established a home, Tolstoy Farms, for the Satyagrahis who lived in simplicity and with total self-reliance. This was the time when the inmates of the home shunned their British attire.

Mahatma Gandhi went through the second phase of sartorial integrity when he moved to India in 1914. He landed at the Bombay docks wearing a Kathiawadi dress and a dhoti. As he travelled across the country to get first-hand accounts of suffering and poverty, he realized that India must be freed from the clutches of the British Raj. He started the swadeshi movement and pitched in self-reliance with khadi, which could be homespun.

In 1921, while visiting the southern part of the country, he saw ill-clad men and women during a public meeting at Madurai. He decided that he would from then onwards wear only a loincloth and use a 'chaddar' or shawl to cover his body only if required. This was one of the most important and radical sartorial integrity-related decisions taken by him. This became his trademark; Winston Churchill would later refer to him as 'the half-naked fakir'. Gandhi took this as a compliment. He moved from sophisticated British outfits to a loincloth in stages. But he lived by what he thought was right and lived with integrity. He demonstrated what it was to be congruent and authentic.

Integrity in Personal and Work Life

As Alan Simpson, a US senator says, 'If you have integrity, nothing else matters. If you don't have integrity, nothing else matters.'

Today, the world is in transition. One is a witness to much corruption and wrongdoing. Let us not get carried away by saying that this only means that integrity has lost its relevance in today's world. The fact is, it has become all the more important in our personal conduct as well as in a leadership role. Would you employ even an office boy, a domestic help or a driver who is dishonest and falls short on integrity?

In the globalized world, people from developing countries have to deal with developed nations. Each country has different laws, but the 'law of integrity' remains the same across the world. In the world of business, integrity as an issue can never be compromised, regardless of the country you live in. Business houses as well as individuals take years to build a reputation based on credibility, but one wrong act can jeopardize a great reputation.

'Whoever is careless with the truth in small matters cannot be trusted with important matters.'
—Albert Einstein, theoretical physicist

> **LEADERSHIP LESSONS FROM A SAINT WITHOUT AUTHORITY**
>
> 1. Leaders must practise what they preach.
> 2. People will follow you only if you demonstrate integrity and honesty of purpose through your own actions.
> 3. The law of integrity is the same across the world. Wherever one works and whichever country one lives in, integrity can never be compromised.
> 4. Integrity is all about good intentions.

3

ART OF COMMUNICATION
How to Share Your Goals with People

'Truthful words are not beautiful; beautiful words are not truthful. Good words are not persuasive; persuasive words are not good.'
—Lao Tzu, Chinese philosopher

One of the most important qualities of an effective leader is to be able to share his vision and mission with his people. Mahatma Gandhi had a difficult task of reaching out to 30 million Indians who spoke different languages, had diverse subcultures, castes and religious beliefs. Unlike contemporary leaders, he did not have the benefit of mass media like radio or television in those days. But he was a good leader, one who understood these challenges and found innovative solutions in order to effectively reach out to people across the country.

The three essential requirements to reach your audience include the following:

- Content: This is all the material, facts, and figures, related to your topic or to the message that you want to convey to your target audience.

- Ability to articulate: This requires the proper structuring of one's thoughts in a logical manner. It requires clarity of thought as well as fluent and clear speech.
- Command over language: This includes style, voice modulation, and diction.

It is important to understand that command over language gives you the ability of 'How to say', while it is also important to focus on content which is about 'What to say'. Most people lay more emphasis on diction and style and miss out on the substance. Gandhi himself was not a great orator. But he had a very clear philosophy and thought around which he built an argument.

Gandhi did not resort to rhetoric but instead stuck to sincerity of purpose. As a mass leader, he walked the extra mile by demonstrating credibility, honesty and consistency, while communicating his point of view. This enabled him to touch the hearts of millions. He understood that in an uprising against the British Raj, the involvement of every Indian had to be at the emotional level. He spoke from his heart and that compensated for his lack of outstanding oratorical style.

Another important aspect of Mahatma Gandhi's communication skills was his personal conviction. Anyone who heard him was convinced about his authenticity. His audiences felt that he was always telling the truth and that he meant what he said. He was passionate about his purpose and he wore it on his sleeve.

Ability to Connect with a Heterogeneous Audience

Gandhi's simplistic approach appealed to the rural masses, slum dwellers and the illiterate as well as semi-literate populace of India of those days. He skilfully changed the style and texture of his content while dealing with freedom fighters, the elite, the intellectuals and thinkers. Gandhi spoke English, Hindi, and Gujarati but was revered by even those who did not understand these languages in many parts of the country, like Orissa, Bengal or down South. His was a charismatic leadership which broke the barriers of language.

He communicated with the British with dignity and respect. In fact, this earned him more respect than anybody could imagine. When King George V warned him against attacks on the British empire at a reception at Buckingham Palace in England, Gandhi politely said, 'I must not be drawn into a political argument in Your Majesty's palace after such hospitality.'

He had an uncanny way of conveying his point at the right time, to the right person in the right way. This is something every leader must learn.

Forthright and Fearless

Gandhi was very courageous to speak his mind and express his opinions. He was sincere, direct and clear about his philosophy. He would neither mince nor sugarcoat his words and instead always spoke genuinely from his heart.

For instance, after the partition of the country, when Winston Churchill made a critical remark regarding the post-Independence riots and massacre that had erupted, Gandhi rebuked the British prime minister saying, 'If Mr Churchill knew that India would be reduced to such a state after Independence, did he realize that the entire responsibility for this lies with the British Empire?'

Gandhi was also very passionate about his purpose and

philosophy. He was fearless even when he addressed his own people and never spared the rod. In April 1921, speaking against untouchability, he wrote in a daily newspaper: 'Hinduism has sinned in giving sanction to untouchability.' Any other Hindu would have probably avoided such harsh words against fellow Hindus, so as not to offend them. On another occasion he said, 'The curse of foreign domination and the attendant exploitation is the justest retribution meted out by God to us for our exploitation of a sixth of our Race in the sacred name of religion… We are guilty of having suppressed our brethren, we make them crawl on their bellies, make them rub their noses on ground… What more than this has the British rule done to us?'

The most important thing to learn from Gandhi is to be sincere, direct and clear while communicating your thoughts.

Gandhi, because of his conviction, his courage and plainspeak, could reach out and relate to people of diverse backgrounds. He understood his audience and realized the complexity of his task to address Hindus, Muslims, Christians and Sikhs who had different religious, beliefs, customs and their own myths.

Communication and Purpose

Most people, while drafting their speeches or preparing a presentation, tend to forget these basic requirements for effective speaking: what is the purpose of this talk? Is it convincing enough?

Gandhi knew that colonialism was the stepping stone for nationalism and that India's diverse populace would unite and rally around only one point and that was 'Swaraj' or self-rule. He made this the convincing purpose around which the entire independence movement was later built. The purpose of Swaraj was so compelling for every Indian, regardless of his caste, colour, religion, or language, that when Gandhi spoke in places in Bengal or Orissa where Hindi was not even understood, women still donated their ornaments in response to his call. In addition, if the purpose appeals at an emotional level, it has a much greater impact. The call for Swaraj had a similar emotional impact on all the Indians from north to south and from east to west. Gandhi understood the pain and anguish of the Indian masses, their feelings and their emotions at that point in time. It was so appealing that even those Indians who were serving the British government contributed to the movement, some of them albeit hesitatingly.

When Gandhi spoke to the grass-roots, he spoke of untouchability, khadi, self sufficiency and self respect. He knew the evils of alcohol and its negative impact on families, especially in the rural areas. Therefore he talked about eradication of alcohol.

Sacrifices for a Higher Purpose

If a leader has lofty aims and can demonstrate a higher purpose to his audience, he can expect spectacular results. In our day-to-day existence, money and material needs become the driving force. If one looks at armed forces across the world, their mottos revolve around 'Service before Self', 'Country First' or 'Honour, Duty, Country'. These are apparently intangible, but very effective view points to motivate people. These are lofty aims with a compelling purpose which can motivate people to even give their lives. Independence is all about honour and country, which motivates every individual. The crux of communication is to connect your goals with a higher purpose.

Mahatma and his Metaphors

Way back in 323 BC, Aristotle said, 'The greatest thing by far is to be a master of metaphor. It is one thing that cannot be learnt from others.' He goes on to say that it is also a sign of genius, since a good metaphor implies an eye for resemblance. Mahatma Gandhi showed such genius: he created his own lexicon, his own vocabulary, his metaphoric expressions and used them very effectively.

'Swaraj', for instance, was a word around which Gandhi developed a whole philosophy, one of self-governance. It was closely related with 'azadi' or 'independence' by every single Indian. It stressed on discarding everything that was British. According to him the raison d'etre of a state was not governance but serving the people. He called the state a 'soulless machine' which harmed the people. That is why he came up with ideas like 'bhoodan' and that was the beginning of the end of the feudal zamindari system in India.

Gandhi's idea of establishing a Ram Rajya was an extension of Swaraj—a raj which would be based on goodwill, honesty, and caring for one and all. He coined the word 'Harijan' for the untouchables so that they had a more dignified name. Khadi, meanwhile, was a symbol for self-reliance and simplicity. Other terms that caught on with the youth like wildfire were 'non-cooperation' and 'Quit India'.

Through his metaphoric lexicon, Gandhi sold Indians a dream, a hope and something to fight for. Gandhi in fact gave the world its most potent metaphor, three wise monkeys, to say, 'See no evil, hear no evil and speak no evil.'

The Power of the Pen

Mahatma Gandhi, from his early days in South Africa where he started his struggle against the British Raj, realized that 'the pen is mightier than the sword'. He discovered that in order to reach out to the masses and shape public opinion, tools for mass communication, such as a newspaper, were necessary. Thus he started a paper called the *Indian Opinion* in South Africa and became its editor. Then he published *Young India*, a weekly paper from 1919–32. Later, he came out with another weekly called *Harijan* which was published till 1948 in English, Hindi and Gujarati. For almost forty years Gandhi used journalism in his battle against the British Raj. Through his philosophy of life he defined some very important goal posts for modern journalism. He believed, for instance, that the objectives of a newspaper are to arouse people's sentiments, to give expression to their feelings and fearlessly expose the defects of the system. He was also of the firm opinion that a newspaper should not be started for profit; rather, the primary aim of a newspaper is public service and if it is to generate money, it will result in serious malpractices and corruption. To demonstrate his commitment to his cause he wrote what he felt was right and showed courage in the face of adversity.

Every leader must make use of the 'tool of the day' for communication. Gandhi used the newspaper because that was what was available at that time. Adolf Hitler and Winston Churchill used the print media as well as radio throughout the Second World War to remain in touch with their people.

Leaders must therefore learn to identify contemporary communication tools and use them to reach out to their audience. Today, social media has gone far ahead of electronic media. It has a global presence and must be used effectively by every leader. When an orator also becomes a writer, then that leader turns into a complete commentator.

Leaders with the Same Purpose but Different Strategies

If one considers contemporary leaders of Mahatma Gandhi's time, two names come to mind: Adolf Hitler and Winston Churchill.

Hitler and Churchill told their people what they wanted to hear. Hitler's entire argument was based on the injustice done to the German people by the Treaty of Versailles after the First World War and the war reparations which were impossible for the Germans to accept. He knew that Germans wanted to engage in a physical battle and win back their honour. He sold them a dream of conquering the world and establishing the Third Reich. Churchill had to lead a country that was about to be defeated in war. His people were in despair and lacked a sense of security. He had to tell them to show tenacity to retain not only their freedom but their very existence.

Gandhi told the opposite of what people wanted to hear. He talked of non-violence, a concept that was new for all. He talked about togetherness, harmony, 'sarvodya' (rise of all) and selflessness. He told people to shun untouchability and treat each one with respect and equally. Gandhi realized that the language of peace and prosperity was more acceptable to the people at large than the language of 'violence and hatred', which was likely to divide people.

Gandhi's conviction of peace and prosperity was so strong and his approach so humble that he wrote a very simple letter to Adolf Hitler in 1939 just before the war, urging him not to wage war against the rest of Europe, as that would lead only to mass destruction and reduce humanity to a savage state. The last sentence of the letter says, '...anyway, I anticipate your forgiveness, if I have erred in writing to you'; Gandhi's humble approach was clear. Unfortunately, the letter never reached Hitler.

Gandhi's Lessons on the Art of Communication

The most important learning is to have a central theme and a compelling argument backed with solid content while communicating with the people. Moreover, the argument must touch an emotional chord wherever possible.

Use of innovative metaphor is an extremely effective way to make an impact. It is the most potent way to make a lasting impression. Using different tools of mass communication is something every individual as well as a leader must realize.

United States President Barack Obama, for instance, used social media extensively during his campaign. The strategy has been cited as one of the major reasons for his victory. US presidential elections also use TV debates as well as radio to reach out to citizens.

The art of communication is something which every leader must work on. This is a continuous process and one has to keep improving day on day, throughout one's life and career.

'Genius is the ability to put into effect what is on your mind.'
—F. Scott Fitzgerald

LEADERSHIP LESSONS FROM A SAINT WITHOUT AUTHORITY

1. The most effective way to convince your audience is to speak from your heart and with conviction.
2. A person must learn to change and tune style as well as content according to the type of audience being addressed.
3. Wherever required, a leader must speak his or her mind out fearlessly.
4. While speaking, you must create a central theme for your address, a compelling idea which becomes the central shaft of your message.
5. A speaker should try to connect the message to a higher purpose or to a noble cause. This is the most effective way to make people follow you.
6. A good communicator makes effective use of metaphor in his or her content.
7. If you want to reach out to your audience, you must use the right media vehicle.

4

THE GANDHIAN PHILOSOPHY

Redefining Non-violence as a Way of Life

'Faith is taking the first step even when you don't see the whole staircase.'
—Martin Luther King, Jr,
African-American activist and humanitarian

Mahatma Gandhi extended the scope of non-violence—an extension of Ahinsa ('to not injure')— and made it a way of life for the ordinary person. Gandhi claimed to be a 'practical idealist' rather than a 'visionary'. He believed that non-violence was not only for saints but also for common people; thus, it required a bit of modification. According to him, non-violence was like a tree for the law of suffering whereas non-cooperation, Satyagraha, renunciation of the material and civil resistance were its logical branches. Instead of merely preaching, Gandhi practised non-violence in order to demonstrate his resolve to the cause. In his practice he wanted to be fully truthful, fully non-violent in thought, word and deed. To develop what later became popular as 'Gandhian philosophy', he banked heavily on the religions of the world. He took the best of each religion and interpreted it to fit his scheme. Since his own thought process was very clear, and was backed by an extremely strong conviction, it was easy for him to grasp a lot of true value from each faith.

Power of Religion and Faith

All religions came into being because they were profoundly appealing to the masses. Each religious philosophy was timeless and therefore their preachings were as good as eternal. People across religions have been donating to religious organizations for centuries. In 2012, in the US alone, religious organizations received more than $300 billion as charity.

As Gandhi said, religion is a concept of the brave. All prophets, therefore, went through demonstrated sufferings: Lord Ram, Gautam Buddha, Mahavir or the Sikh gurus, all took upon themselves a difficult path, one of suffering and sacrifice. Names of these gurus have been chanted for thousands of years. It is not surprising then, that it would be difficult to recollect the name of the seventh president of the United States (Andrew Jackson) or the prime minister of England during the First World War (David Lloyd George); both of them wielded tremendous power during their time. But in comparison the entire world will be able to relate Buddhism with Gautam Buddha even 2,600 years after his death. Gandhi believed that non-violence was the common factor for all religions, though each religion treats it in different measures, some less and some more. But he also warned that non-violence was not to be used as a cloak for cowardice.

Gandhi's Learning from Hinduism

Gandhi was born Hindu but was respectful to all other religions. He knew that every religion had something wonderful to offer. He once said, 'I am proud to belong to that Hinduism which is all-inclusive and which stands for tolerance.' He believed that such an open concept-based religion would last as long as the sun shone. According to him his Hinduism included the best of Christianity, Buddhism, Zoroastrianism and Islam. He approached politics and his struggle against discrimination in a religious spirit. He also had strong reservations against the caste system which was part of Hinduism. In fact he was the biggest change agent to get India out of the caste system. He was pained at how upper-caste Hindus had ill-treated the lower castes, for centuries.

Buddhism as an Extension of Hinduism

As Protestantism in Christianity is to Catholicism, Buddhism is to Hinduism. Hinduism is beyond a religion, it is a way of life. It is seen as the oldest living tradition on earth, with its foundations going back into the prehistoric era. It is inherently flexible, accommodating and tolerant. Nevertheless, over time the Hindu way of living became a bit too rigid, probably at the dictates of the priests and the keepers. Gautam Buddha, around 600 BC, came into the world when Hinduism was going through this changed stance of rigidity. When the Buddha was pained by human suffering, for which the root cause was humans themselves, he decided to change things. He taught that everyone is equal and therefore the practice of untouchability and casteism was to be demolished. He preached non-violence or Ahinsa and advocated the path of love. Born to a Hindu king, he left the comforts of a kingdom in search of the truth. He realized that attachment causes the greatest pain and suffering to humans and therefore preached a path of renunciation and detachment. Instead of treating life as a bundle of joy and privileges, one should treat it like a bundle of duties, devotion and service to others, and that is what he practised. Gandhi hailed Buddha as the preserver and saviour of Hinduism by breaking down bad traditions of Hinduism at that point in history when Hinduism was developing some cracks within. In fact, Gandhi modified the concept of non-violence to give it a larger-than-life meaning, as Buddha modified Hinduism.

Mahatma Gandhi read only a few books on the Buddha. His major learnings were from *The Light of Asia* by Sir Edwin Arnold. But these were enough for him to get the essence of Buddhism which he could imaginatively adapt into his own conviction-based philosophy. He used these principles of 'equality for all' in South Africa and also later in India during the country's freedom struggle.

Jainism for Applied Social Justice

Jainism has its basis in humans being able to conquer their passions, urges and need for bodily pleasures. Ahinsa or non-violence is most radical, comprehensive and to an extent rigorous in Jainism, more than any other religion. 'Ahinsa Parmo Dharma'—meaning 'non-violence is the supreme religion'—was the basis of Jainism as preached by Lord Mahavir, who was the most influential preacher of Jainism around 600 BC. Gandhi once said, 'If anyone has practised to the fullest extent and propagated Ahinsa, it was Lord Mahavir.' In addition to non-violence, Jainism encourages truthfulness and self-control, as well as renunciation of worldly possessions.

Like Hinduism, Jainism also promotes fasting, and a pure vegetarian diet devoid of many vegetables that grow below the ground, or root vegetables. Being one of the purest and most elaborately defined vegetarian diets, which does not allow onions and garlic, it is very rigorous and people may find it extremely difficult to follow it fully in letter and in spirit.

Gandhi adopted 'Ahinsa Parmo Dharma' almost completely and yet pragmatically into his form of non-violence. He made things more doable. In fact, he was the first one to use the principles of Jainism for the pursuit of societal upliftment and social justice. He made things more practical and wide-based in their applicability.

In this context, Gandhi realized that we do need to destroy as much life as we think necessary for sustaining our lives and bodies. He went on to say that 'we may destroy termites and mosquitoes by use of disinfectants and may resort to kill a carnivorous beast to protect ourselves'. He thus embraced the essence of Jainism but moved away from its rigidity. Gandhi gave non-violence a larger meaning by his concept of 'absence of hatred'. He said that by prayers and discipline he managed to abandon hate for almost forty years. His non-cooperation had its roots in love and not hatred. He said, 'Love people but hate evil'; we cannot be non-violent and yet have hatred inside us. He believed that forgiveness is more difficult than punishment and therefore forgiving is more manly than punishing someone. Jainism does not encourage use of vehicles, therefore Jain monks usually walk to collect 'bhiksha'. Gandhi used vehicles in the normal day-to-day activity, but took up long marches to protest, which he adopted from Jainism. His white clothing was also inspired by Jainism, as white defines simplicity and purity.

Lessons from Sikhism and Christianity

Gandhi always looked at the Sikh religion as an offshoot of Hinduism. It came into existence to protect Hindus and Hinduism. Though a perfectly noble reason, it was not appreciated by some Sikhs as the Sikh religion had much more to offer than merely protecting Hinduism. Sikhism also had some major tenets that fully matched with Gandhi's own philosophy: Sikh gurus preached that all human races are equal, women have equal status and rights and salvation can be attained by meditating on God.

In Christianity Gandhi found the concept of forgiveness and redemption through sacrifice quite appealing. Redemption means to buy back, and you can buy back salvation only through giving up something, which is self-sacrifice. Jesus giving up his life on the cross without hatred for those who sinned, appealed to Mahatma Gandhi.

Looking at almost all the religions of the world, not one of them preaches violence or hatred. And Mahatma Gandhi, having studied most religions, firmed up his own Gandhian philosophy. He remains widely regarded as the greatest prophet of the twentieth century.

Buddhism, Gandhi and the Caste System

Gandhi was as pained about the caste system—especially untouchability, being practised by Hindus—as was Gautam Buddha. While Buddha took it forward in the name of religion, Gandhi sought to make it a national and political movement and was largely successful because his movement culminated into a nation state. Finally in 1950, the national Constitution of India abolished untouchability.

The caste system, however, was so deeply rooted in the Indian psyche that it was very difficult to get rid of it even after Independence. The caste system has managed to permanently alter the DNA of Indian people. Couples married in the same caste carried this tradition forward, and some still do. If one examines it closely, then largely the 'look and feel' of a Brahmin is different than that of a Kshatriya. Similarly, a Vaishya would be different from a Brahmin. Look and feel would imply features, complexion, height, weight and body structure. This was further aggravated due to lifestyles and food habits of people in different castes, which is scientifically known as epigenetics. To complicate things further, more sub-castes or 'jatis' emerged within each of the four major castes.

Gandhian Non-violence in Our Daily Lives

In our daily lives we experience problems and seemingly impossible obstacles. One doesn't have to start an agitation against smaller problems but one can use 'non-violence' as a basic principle for dealing with people and situations.

Leaders must view non-violence more pragmatically and broadly and try to adapt the philosophy according to the need of the hour. Sun Tzu, the Chinese philosopher and author of the famous work, *The Art of War*, written around 2,500 years ago, also stressed the fact that 'war is a necessary evil that must be avoided whenever possible.' Diplomacy, in fact, stems from non-violence. If you can convince your opponent across the table that what he is doing is not right and there exists a better method based on dialogue, or give and take, then a physical or a violent conflict can be avoided. War is waged when other options have run out. It is also important to understand and estimate the strength of the opponent as compared to your own. In business studies a SWOT analysis (Strengths, Weaknesses, Opportunities, and Threats) is resorted to in every situation where one has to estimate the ability of the organization within the business environment.

Many thinkers are of the view that non-violence is the best weapon for the weaker party. If your opponent is physically stronger than you—which the British were as compared to the Indian freedom fighters—then non-violence becomes an extremely potent weapon.

In business, similarly, if a SWOT analysis reveals that the opponent is much stronger than you, it is better to look at options other than direct confrontation. A non-violent approach also draws public sympathy and everybody else supports your cause. One must apply non-violence to ultimately achieve one's goals. The strategy thus needs to be well-thought out from end to end.

Gandhi knew that to obtain freedom from the British a movement, however massive, would not be enough. It required a political body which would eventually govern the country once the British left. Thus in 1915 he joined the Indian National Congress and became its president. As they say, the rest is history.

Social activist, Anna Hazare, meanwhile, started his agitation against the government in 2011 much along the lines of Gandhian principles of fasting 'Jail Bharo' (fill the jails), and non-violence. He led movements to promote rural development, increase government transparency and investigate and punish official corruption. He failed to give it a political shape, though, without which freedom from corruption was not possible for

India. That is why despite so much public support the entire effort was lost in the din. You cannot bring change sitting at Jantar Mantar; the right place is the Parliament and for that, Anna Hazare should have given his movement a political shape.

It was clear that Mahatma Gandhi had a keen sense of his movement's political significance. Gandhi, moreover, had a very high emotional quotient (EQ). One proof of this is that in order to understand the ground realities he travelled across India and met people from all strata of society. Only then did he feel the pulse of the Indian people. Gandhi thus demonstrated the art of 'social intelligence gathering' before this concept was even conceived in EQ jargon.

Business leaders must walk the corridors and meet people at all levels—especially the workforce—to get the feel not only of the organization as a bigger picture but of the ranks as well. Then the task of connecting with the organization becomes easier.

Negotiation is yet one instrument which, in my opinion, is an offshoot of the non-violent approach. The principle of negotiation is never to say, 'Take it or leave it'—this in a way is an aggressive approach bordering on violence, at least in thought. It is good to negotiate hard-softly, rather than ending up with a softer negotiation pushing the harder way.

Moreover, on the interpersonal level, the principles of emotional intelligence encourage a more humane approach rather than a brash one.

I remember attending an annual general meeting of our residential society where issues regarding security were being heatedly debated. There was a complaint against a young man, who was accused of being rude to the security guards almost every day. The members attending this meeting wanted the secretary of the society to summon the young man to the meeting and rebuke him publicly right then and there.

The secretary, who obviously was behaving more maturely, did summon the young man. He did not rebuke him, though, and instead made a very humble request for him to be a part of the security committee of the society. He said, 'Young man, if you do not help us in maintaining our own security, then who will?' When he said this in front of all the members, this young man was taken aback, as he was expecting to be scolded for his rude behaviour. This, to me, was a clear case of how non-aggressive, non-violent behaviour can help find a solution even at the individual level.

Business leaders must learn from Gandhi's approach of distilling this essence out of ideas, philosophies and approaches presented to them. They must keep their minds open and study the relevant content, which is useful to resolving the problem at hand, and then take the kernel out and apply it in the best possible way. Gandhi did this all the time by studying different religions, and taking the best from each one of them to come up with his own philosophy. This is the most important aspect of leadership, especially at the top levels, where policy issues are to be addressed. Interpretation of philosophy is more important than the philosophy itself.

Reading a story is knowledge, but understanding the moral of the story is wisdom and putting that wisdom into practice is pragmatic leadership. Charity, for instance, has a very large applicability. All religions preach charity but how each one of us takes it up may differ. Many people look at charity from the religious point of view. Therefore they make temples in the name of God or give donations to a church or gurudwara; some others give food and clothes to the poor. Some open hospitals or schools. Today a lot of charity is done for research to find a cure for dreaded diseases.

Ultimately it boils down to interpretation of a philosophy, an idea or a narrative according to one's own convictions. Gandhi did exactly that throughout his life.

'What is magnificent about humans is when they decide to turn and stand. If they respond with non-violence on principle and hold their ground, they are really magnificent.'

—James Cromwell

LEADERSHIP LESSONS FROM A SAINT WITHOUT AUTHORITY

1. Leaders should have a lofty vision but they should be able to translate this into simple words, so that the junior-most individual in the organization or their target audience should be able to understand and implement that vision.
2. One must study philosophies, viewpoints and ideas of great people from which valuable lessons can be culled. The essence of good leadership lies in interpreting these ideas and intelligently adapting their essence according to your needs.
3. Diplomacy is the cheapest option to handle any situation. Aggression, fighting or declaring a war on your opponent is the costliest way to resolve a dispute. Therefore diplomacy, which is another form of non-violence, should be resorted to for resolving any issues or points of confrontation.
4. If your opponent is stronger than you, non-violence is the best method to adopt.
5. Leaders must constantly monitor the pulse of the masses and their teams, and their people. They must keep interacting with people and remain constantly updated on the social intelligence front.
6. It is good to develop the art of negotiation. It pays in the long run.

5

THOUGHT LEADERS NEED AN EXTERNAL COMPASS

People, Personalities and Philosophies

> *'If I have seen further than others, it is by standing upon the shoulders of giants.'*
> —Isaac Newton, physicist and mathematician

Every individual is influenced by various external factors. We may be influenced by our parents, for example, or by our teachers, and even friends. To a large extent these factors help mould our personality and character and, sometimes, even our destiny.

Leaders who attain responsible positions and who bring about changes within their radius of influence develop their own styles of working and a certain belief system based on a philosophy. In modern management parlance such people are termed as 'thought leaders'. Such leaders also get inspired and influenced not only by people and personalities but also by literature and religious philosophies. A thinking leader eventually needs to discuss his ideas with other intellects to give shape to his own ideas and beliefs. He needs to discuss with like-minded people in order to reinforce his own convictions. In essence, a leader cannot progress in a vacuum and all these sources of intellect are like oxygen for him.

Mahatma's Quest for Truth:
Literary Figures Who Influenced Gandhi

Gandhi's journey started as a lawyer in 1891 once he reached India after finishing his studies in England. He started practising law with disastrous results, as he found it difficult to make both ends meet as a start-up lawyer in Bombay. He immediately accepted an offer to work for a law firm in South Africa. Thus began the journey that was to eventually lead to his life's mission. South Africa was to become the flash point of the world's clash of colour and Gandhi was destined to be at the centre of that storm.

European whites who had settled in that country treated non-whites very badly. Indians were labelled as coolies (labourers) regardless of their qualifications or profession, so there were coolie teachers, coolie lawyers and coolie businessmen. Gandhi's first bitter experience of discrimination was when he was thrown out of a first-class compartment on to the platform with his luggage. He thereafter witnessed rampant discrimination which was being legalized by unjust laws, written by the whites in their own favour.

Instead of returning to India, he decided to fight racial injustice. This was the beginning, the first phase of Gandhi's political career, the second phase being his struggle to obtain independence for India. The foundation of his philosophy and political thought was based on his experience in South Africa.

He received his initial lessons and his spiritual nourishment from his supporters and friends as well as philosophers in the decade that he spent in this country. His time in South Africa was to shape his convictions and values for a lifetime. It was like a crucible for experimenting and formulating his own philosophy.

By confronting bigger problems which seem to have no solution, you are in a way trying to create history. Gandhi was up against such a problem and he could not create history alone or in a vacuum.

When Gandhi was taking a decision to stay in South Africa to fight against discrimination, he read *Letter to a Hindoo* by Leo Tolstoy. This was a letter Tolstoy had written in response to C.R. Das, a revolutionary representative of Indians in England, who was against the philosophy of non-violent resistance, propagated by Tolstoy. Gandhi was so impressed by this letter that he asked for Tolstoy's permission to publish it in South Africa. In fact this was the beginning of a rich correspondence between the two great minds, which was to become a landmark in the history of novel ideas and actionable philosophy of the future. *The Kingdom of God is Within You,* a book also written by Tolstoy, left an abiding and lasting impression on the young Gandhi. Tolstoy in this book had portrayed how an authentic Christian life is to be led and looked at Christ more as a teacher rather than a godly saviour of mankind. Almost three decades later, Gandhi said, 'Russia gave me in Tolstoy, a teacher who furnished a reasoned basis for my non-violence movement in South Africa, whose wonderful possibilities I had yet to learn. He even prophesied that I was moving on the right lines and would bring hope to the downtrodden people of the earth.'

Another author who made a deep impression on Gandhi was John Ruskin. Gandhi read his book, *Unto This Last*, on a train journey from Johannesburg to Durban in 1904, and was so moved that it kept him awake in the night. Gandhi firmed up his political economic thought based on three points described by Ruskin in his book: that the good of the individual is in the good of all; a lawyer's work has the same value as a barber's and everybody else's, regardless of the occupation, everyone has the same right of earning a livelihood; and it is worth living the life of a tiller of the soil as a labour. Gandhi, after reading the book realized that the first of the three tenets he already knew, the second he dimly realized, but the third one had never occurred to him! He later used these principles and put them into practice during the course of his freedom struggle. He also translated it into Gujarati and called it 'Sarvodya', meaning 'progress for all'. Gandhi was also influenced by the Gita and the Bible and could draw some important lessons from these two holy scriptures.

Influential Figures

In the course of his leadership of the freedom struggle, Gandhi was influenced by various individuals. Among them was his political guru, Gopal Krishna Gokhale; Gandhi called him his 'mentor guide'. He described Gokhale as 'the Ganga in which one could have a refreshing holy bath'. No wonder Gandhi banked on him for advice whenever he was in a difficult situation. Gandhi's spiritual guru, meanwhile, was Shrimad Rajchandra, whom he met in Mumbai soon after his return from England. He was also known as Raichand Bhai, a Jain philosopher who shaped up Gandhi's idea of Ahinsa and spirituality.

Gandhi also drew upon history to sound-board his own philosophy. When he started his struggle against racial discrimination of Indians in South Africa, he had to convince Indians to be ready for sacrifice and pain in order to fight for their rights and for the sake of truth. Gandhi chose Socrates as an example, the ancient Greek philosopher whom he called 'a soldier of truth'. He told people to follow Socrates's example because he fought for the truth and all his accusers and judges of his time stand condemned even today. Gandhi emphasized the need for Satyagrahis to learn to live and die like Socrates.

As far as political philosophy is concerned, Gandhi and Tolstoy both believed that the abolition of the state was necessary to realize social and economic equity. They both talked about non-possession. Even Karl Marx and Vladimir Lenin believed in revolution but one that was based on force, rather than non-violence.

Influence of Different Religions

Gandhi was open to consider all philosophies and accepted those that were close to his conscience and appealed to his logic.

Buddhism and Jainism appealed to him because they preached Ahinsa, which prohibits the killing of any living being. As mentioned earlier, Jainism is an absolute staunch supporter of Ahinsa whereas Buddhism is a little more flexible. That is why Buddhist monks joined armies and served as soldiers in Japan, China, and Korea. Jainism promotes absolute Ahinsa, while Buddhism preaches 'Maitri' (friendliness) and 'Karuna' (Compassion). Gandhi defined Ahinsa in a little more practical and realistic way—possibly an amalgamation of both, leading to a middle path. He held a view that 'all killing is not hinsa'; he said, for example, that rabid dogs and poisonous snakes may have to be killed if they threaten life. Gandhi's Ahinsa was flexible and reactive; it was not absolute.

Lessons for Business Leaders

To be an effective leader who wants to bring about change and demolish the status quo, it is essential to have a compelling reason. That reason can be viewed as the problem for which s/he seeks a solution. The solution lies in a philosophy-based strategy which gradually turns into a series of actions to solve the problem.

For instance, a compelling reason for a political leader would be the well-being and freedom of countrymen. For the chief executive officer (CEO) of a failing company, the turnaround of the organization becomes a compelling reason. For the chief marketing officer (CMO), that reason is meeting sales targets for products in a competitive market.

Just as Gandhi, in order to bring freedom for his countrymen, had a philosophy-based strategy of non-cooperation through Satyagraha and non-violence, a CEO who needs to turn around a sick unit may look at discipline, instilling responsiveness in employees and quality of manpower as a philosophy-based strategy to bring about a change.

After all, it is what separates the great leaders from the good leaders: the great ones come up with a workable, and many times unique, philosophy-based strategy to solve the problem. Therefore philosophy is in essence at the centre of it. To arrive at a reasonably good philosophy, a leader needs sources of inspiration, some past precedents, if any, to sound-board upon and some mentors to learn from.

To help senior management to perform more effectively, executive coaches do a wonderful job. They act like paid mentors and help business leaders to not only hone their skills but also provide valuable inputs to find solutions to complex problems.

Business leaders more often than not also come across mentors at their workplace. These are people whom they can trust and who usually have more experience than the mentee himself. One of the dictionary definitions of the word mentor is 'A wise trusted counsellor'. Mentoring is usually one-on-one. Effective bosses can act like teachers or mentors to their immediate subordinates, in order to help them achieve their goals.

Books are those so-called 'philosophy triggers' which are hard to ignore. A book can change one's life and can have a deep impact on one's philosophy towards life and work. Leaders must read inspirational books of different genres, written by thinkers and practising leaders. If one can pick up three good points from a book, it is already worth the effort.

Last but not the least, religions play a very important part in business leadership roles, like they did for Gandhi. A sense of charity and philosophy for instance can well stem out of faith in Christianity, Hinduism or Islam. Great or the greatest business leaders draw upon different religions to ultimately firm up their own philosophy of action, as all religions have a lot of wisdom to share.

'Let each man take the path according to his capacity, understanding and temperament. His true guru will meet him along that path.'
—Sivananda Saraswati

LEADERSHIP LESSONS FROM A SAINT WITHOUT AUTHORITY

1. As a leader, you must have a compelling reason to start a new venture or a project.
2. As an individual, or a leader, you must read books written by great authors. They can trigger new ideas and mould your thinking for a positive change.
3. You must meet and interact with knowledgeable people as they have a lot to offer in terms of knowledge and ideas.
4. Try and take on a few people as your mentors and guides. Mature advice is something very precious; coming from gurus and mentors, it can have a positive effect on your way of working.

6

FROM 'KAUN' TO ICON

360-degree Brand Building, the Gandhi Way

'Your premium brand had better be delivering something special, or it's not going to get the business.'

—Warren Buffett, business magnate

Philosophy-based Branding

Mahatma Gandhi is probably one of the biggest brand icons of the twentieth century. He is revered across the world, more than sixty-five years after his death. As years pass, it seems as if the value of this iconic brand is ever increasing rather than diminishing. It is worth examining as to how a frail man, with no authority and with no resources at his command, could make an impact on billions of people at home and abroad. This in fact is the ultimate test a leader has to pass.

Gandhi's biggest plus point was how he did things differently. 'My life is my message,' such was his principle, and people were convinced. One could extend this statement by saying, 'His ways were his brand and his actions or karma was his way.' His action-based philosophy was highly grounded and appealed to the masses at an emotional level. Branding as a technique works best when it touches the emotional chord of the target audience. And emotional impact is long lasting, in fact, everlasting. Gandhi appeared as a positive role model; positivity and hope always sells.

It is intriguing that many before and after Gandhi preached and practised non-violence, but none were as successful as him. He coupled discrimination and injustice with nationalism and therefore could convince every section, every religion of society to join him. Gandhi, his concept, his movement, his non-violence, projected him as an underdog. People applaud Hannibal who defeated superior Roman forces at the Battle of Cannae. Mohammad Ali, a newcomer in boxing, became a hero when he defeated Sony Liston who appeared to be undefeatable. If the mighty British Empire was the Goliath, Gandhi for his people was David, who could ultimately come out as the victor. It is the underdog that often gets the public sympathy at an emotional level.

I would like to draw a parallel between Hinduism and Gandhism. Hinduism is a way of life; from waking up to the time we go to bed. Rituals, beliefs, methods, traditions which were loosely structured remained with us always and every time. Similarly, Gandhism defined a way of life as lived by Mahatma Gandhi. Simplicity, Ahinsa, frugal ways, self-reliance, self-control, food habits, and absolute integrity—this was his religion: Gandhism. Hinduism has lasted for long and so will Gandhism.

Ability to Demonstrate Commitment

Gandhi's biggest plus point was his ability to demonstrate his preachings. Most leaders with lofty aims and grand plans fail on this account. But Gandhi had a strong willpower and once he decided on something, there was no way anyone could dissuade him. He was an action leader who could demonstrate his conviction, his passion and his morals as well as dogged determination by his deeds. In modern corporate parlance this is called 'walking the talk'.

There was a time when Gandhi decided not to have cow's milk, after discovering that when a cow is milked, the milking does not stop until the last drop is extracted, causing pain to the animal.

He did not touch milk until he was sixty years old, when doctors forced him to have some as his health was failing. He agreed to have milk, but that of a goat, and not a cow.

Packaging Matters the Most

One may have a great product or a great idea as a product, but unless the packaging is the true representative of the product, it will be difficult to sell it. Gandhi wanted to be 'one of them' for the Indian diaspora. He adopted simplicity in his entire way of life. In England, as a student of law, he had taken pride in wearing well-stitched expensive English suits, shirts and hats. He carried forward the same tempo when he reached South Africa and dressed up well like an upbeat lawyer in South African courts. He brought about a change in his outlook quite gradually yet very consciously. On one occasion during his protest in South Africa, he even shaved off his hair to demonstrate 'mourning'.

Eventually he projected himself as a nondescript, frail and simple person from head to toe. He backed up his belief—'Simple living and high thinking'—by what he wore. He could inspire others because he himself demonstrated what he preached.

Once Gandhi visited a Sevagram Ashram and noticed that the hostel in-charge was wearing a shirt with his top three buttons open. Gandhi asked him why he was wasting cloth. The hostel in-charge could not understand so Gandhi continued, 'People wear clothes to cover their bodies but I can see half of your body. You should either button up your shirt or wear a dhoti like me.' The next day that person wore a loincloth.

When Gandhi arrived in Mumbai (known earlier as Bombay) from South Africa, he wore a Kathiwadi dress consisting of a shirt, a cloak, a dhoti and a simple white scarf, all made of Indian mill cloth. After travelling far and wide in India and seeing the poverty there he was further convinced that no reform was possible unless some of the rich and educated people accepted the ways of the poor by dressing like them, eating in a frugal manner and travelling in third class.

He settled in his Satyagraha Ashram on the outskirts of Ahmedabad in Gujarat because it was a handloom centre and he wanted to kickstart the ancient Indian cottage industry, which he did with his 'charkha' or spinning wheel. He taught people to clothe themselves with cloth made with their own hands. He created khadi, a type of cotton cloth which he, along with all his followers, started wearing.

In one of his motivational campaigns, while he was moving from house to house, he had to wear a pith hat or 'sola topi' to avoid a heat stroke; it was British attire. Some people then criticized him for wearing something British. Gandhi then came up with a khadi-made cap which was later to become a popular pan-India symbol of simplicity; it would be called a

'Gandhi topi'. Again, due to his strong resolve he created something which became a symbol for Indian political leaders and his movement against the British.

Gandhi started wearing a loincloth, to demonstrate that a person 'can live with the minimum'. Only when it became cold did he use a thick 'chaddar' which was nothing but a plain white sheet of cloth. For footwear he wore chappals and for indoors he used wooden 'khadaon'. He wore typical rounded glasses and always carried his small prayer book. As he grew older he used a lathi or a simple walking stick for support when it was required, such as during his long marches.

That is all Gandhi had as his personal possessions. This gave him an immediate connection with the Indian masses. This is what made him a brand, one that oozed simplicity and yet demonstrated a strong resolve to fight. No wonder that after his death, his various personal belongings have fetched thousands of rupees in auctions.

A Brand in Action

Gandhi wanted to prove his point with his deeds. He amply demonstrated that he lived in a frugal manner. The lesson: it is not enough to have the right packaging; the product must perform and speak for itself.

One of the most demonstrative parts of Gandhi's lifestyle was his simple diet. He emphasized on being in harmony with nature as far as possible. He became a pure vegetarian and preferred to have raw vegetables and fruits as a substantial part of his meals. He preferred jaggery over sugar and drank goat's milk, which has its own medical benefits. Gandhi believed that 'man becomes what he eats'. This was said by him much before detailed research linked diet to human behaviour. Now it is well proven that a vegetarian diet not only is good for health but also helps in keeping one's mind calm. He was a frugal eater and had a minimalistic approach to diet.

For Gandhi, fasting had two aspects: it helped clean the body's system and prevented overload on the metabolism; and second, it helped build strong willpower by self-denial. He later on used fasting or 'unshun' as a strong political tool. Once you resort to fasting, it puts adequate psychological pressure on the opponent and also gets you public sympathy. To my mind, fasting was a major brand-building exercise for not only Mahatma Gandhi but also for the entire Indian freedom movement.

Gandhi even used his daily routine as a message to his followers. He had a fixed routine about which he was firm. He stayed in Sevagram Ashram for close to eight years and he rarely budged from his routine. He rose early in the morning at 4 a.m. and finished his community prayers and some writing. By 7 a.m. he had breakfast, went for a walk, helped in the kitchen and cleaned the bathrooms. At 8.30 he met visitors for an hour. He was regular with his oil massage in the sunlight. He also regularly worked on his charkha in the afternoon and had early dinner which he finished by 6 p.m., followed by prayers and a walk. He would then retire by 9 at night.

Gandhi purposely made some extraordinary gestures which amazed his followers. One such incident is related to losing an expensive pen. Gandhi was fond of a fountain pen which he used frequently for his correspondence. As we all often lose our writing instruments, one time Gandhi also lost his. He immediately decided that he would not use anything that was expensive. He started using a pen holder and a nib. This had its own problems and one day the nib got bent. Someone went to get a new nib from the market and Gandhi was upset as precious time was being wasted. Instead of waiting for the nib to arrive, he started sharpening the other end of the wooden holder! He started using that as a nib, declaring that now the point of this nib would never get bent again. He also said that this would improve his handwriting and at no cost.

Learning Brand-building from the Mahatma

Mahatma Gandhi, I should presume, had never planned to make himself into a 'brand' as such. He hired neither a brand manager nor an image consultant. He gradually evolved as an icon. There are a lot of powerful brand management principles one can learn from his journey.

Omnipresence and Building an Identity

To ensure omnipresence, you need to create clones. For Gandhi, in order to ensure his presence across the country, he used the khadi and Gandhi topi as symbols. All his followers used khadi clothing and wore a Gandhi topi. For convenience, some wore pajama kurta instead of a dhoti kurta, but always white. This became a de facto uniform for the Gandhian movement; it replicated his presence across the country. If one would compare this to Hitler's idea of a uniform 'brown shirt' which his stormtroopers or SA used and which he himself wore throughout his rise and fall, one could see a similar pattern. Uniformity builds camaraderie, a strong identity and also an emotional connection that grows deep roots.

Look at contemporary, powerful brands such as McDonald's or Kentucky Fried Chicken or Café Coffee Day: they use the same colour scheme and the same look and feel for all their outlets throughout the world. This is one of the most compelling branding mantras that exists. And imagine, Gandhi did it before brand mantras came into existence in management studies!

A Single Tag Line

It is important for entities to have one tag line which can encapsulate the company's entire philosophy and mission. It should be able to survive for a long period, even be timeless. Gandhi's tag line for himself was succinct and powerful: 'My life is my message.' In the case of Winston Churchill, it was 'V for victory'; this lasted until Britain won the Second World War and has been very often used by leaders and commoners even today. Companies also come up with tag lines for representing themselves and their flagship products. For instance, LG Electronics is a Korean consumer electronics giant which came up after a merger of two companies, Lucky and Gold Star, and hence acquired the abbreviation 'LG'. Later they made it into an 'acronym' for their tagline, 'Life's Good'. Consider Ray Ban, too. At the behest of the US Army, Bausch and Lomb created a type of anti-glare sunglasses that air force pilots could wear to fly in more comfort. Since it prevented or 'banned' the rays of the sun from hurting the eyes, it was called 'Ray Ban': it has since become an iconic brand. For a product or a person, therefore, coming up with a surviving tag line is an essential brand mantra.

To Err is Human, but Can Prove Very Costly

Gandhi, during his journey of life, realized that making a mistake is only human but as one grows in stature one's mistakes get highlighted.

This is a lesson which every leader must remember: a mistake by an icon gets highlighted, especially in today's context, when there is so much of mass media chasing after you. For instance, when former US President Ronald Reagan was caught dozing off during a meeting, it made headlines. The simple act of being tired and thus falling asleep in a meeting became almost unforgivable as it was committed not by an ordinary person but by a president.

Similarly, products manufactured by big companies are always under the media scanner. One error and a scandal erupts. Therefore any hint of negative news becomes big news for companies like Cadbury, Coca Cola or McDonalds. Today, negative publicity can do more damage than good news helping a product.

Make a shock-proof image for your product: An image should be so strong that people swear by it. Gandhi managed to create such an impact on people with his shock-proof image that is intact even today.

Companies like TATA, Infosys, Apple, IBM, or Microsoft have built their respective images which will potentially last for a lifetime. Such images are a culmination of all the above points which need to be in place. People swear by the products of these companies across the globe.

Great innovator for mass publicity: At some point during his ascent to popularity, Gandhi realized the importance of impact and building an image, which in management terms is called 'brand building'. He demonstrated innovation and creativity in every aspect of life to connect with the persona that he actually was, and also as he wanted people to perceive him.

He managed to demonstrate out-of-the-box, innovative thinking in order to achieve 360-degree brand building.

Using Gandhi as a Brand

In politics, people have used Gandhi time and again to appear saintly. Gandhian philosophy, even his attire, have been appropriated by the Congress party (as well as all other political parties) in order to demonstrate that they are as honest as the Mahatma and to therefore form a similar connection with the masses.

Of course, a disconnect immediately surfaces when you see a dhoti-kurta-clad politician getting out of a BMW. Contemporary activists like Anna Hazare have used most of Gandhi's props and methods to catch the attention of the Indian masses and that, too, very successfully. Hazare was successful because he actually has very little personal wealth and lives a simple life.

In the past there have been attempts by some foreign companies to buy the brand 'Gandhi' and use it commercially. This would be truly unacceptable and it is good that the government has never allowed for it. After all, how can one allow the brazen commodification of a national treasure? Gandhi's simplicity and renunciation of the material, by itself, is opposed to the seductive ways of advertising and branding. You simply cannot expect to use Gandhi's name to endorse fancy perfumes or expensive cars: they are all titillating and seductive, the very antithesis to Gandhi's message of simple living. You can, at most, piggyback on the Gandhian philosophy to get an indirect endorsement. Gandhi as a brand is a cultural resource and not a commercial product. It is India's intellectual property and needs to be used very cautiously for a larger purpose.

Mont Blanc, a German luxury goods manufacturer, a few years ago very innovatively launched a fountain pen to pay tribute to Mahatma Gandhi's life and achievements. They cleverly used the colour white to represent truth and peace. The top of the cap and cone are inspired by the spindle (charkha) which Gandhi used to spin cotton. A nice orange garnet is placed on the cap, which represents the Indian flag, and the nib carries the image of Gandhi walking with a stick. With a limited edition of only 3,000, the pens were priced at $ 25,000 or Rs 15 lakh each. They also launched a similar product to pay tribute to Albert Einstein and Alfred Hitchcock, selling them all together as 'the greatest men of the last century'.

'A brand for a company is like a reputation for a person. You earn a reputation by trying to do hard things well.'

—Jeff Bezos, Internet entrepreneur and investor

LEADERSHIP LESSONS FROM A SAINT WITHOUT AUTHORITY

- Individuals, business leaders, as well as organizations can learn a lot from Mahatma Gandhi who single-handedly built an everlasting brand.
- As persons we need to stand out in front of people with our own individuality. Many people today depend on image consultants to enhance their persona. Business leaders make concerted efforts to enhance the brand value of their products as well as their companies. Organizations spend millions towards brand building.
- First of all, whatever image of yourself that you want to project, you must do so with total conviction. It all begins with you believing in yourself and being confident about your product.
- Packaging is the next big thing and it must match with your conviction. Gandhi wanted to shed luxury and this he felt from his heart. Therefore when he spoke about simplicity to others, they became convinced. To demonstrate his resolve he ensured that every part of his attire appeared frugal, every personal possession displayed simplicity.
- Moreover, a product or a person must act according to the projected image. Gandhi's simple vegetarian meals and saintly disciplined life was enough to show that he believed in simple living and high thinking.
- It is important that your product be branded across the desired geographic spread. This is also linked to advertising. For this, innovative replication is required. Using media and manpower, one should

spread the message so as to reach as many people as possible. Gandhi used the media very effectively and by defining a de facto dress code of white khadi, all his followers became his brand ambassadors.
- Create only a few tag lines that are catchy and full of impact. They must address the audience at an emotional level.
- Always keep in mind that to err is human, but the larger the brand, the more vulnerable it becomes to negative publicity. Make sure that you or your products are not caught on the wrong foot. This could prove very costly for a brand you have so painstakingly built over a long time.

7

LEADING FROM THE FRONT
The Mahatma, a Brilliant Organizer

'Lead from the back...and let others believe they are in front.'
—Nelson Mandela, anti-apartheid revolutionary
and former president of South Africa

Mahatma Gandhi led a highly eventful life, starting when he was in South Africa, and later across India. He participated in hundreds of conferences, events, 'yatras', Satyagrahas, public rallies and political meetings, and created various organizations from scratch, with very little money or resources. He could motivate people to voluntarily associate with him, his philosophy and his movement. His followers worked tirelessly and without any monetary rewards. He was ready to experiment and try out new methods, move to difficult locations and yet managed to keep his people together under the most difficult living conditions. His background as a lawyer helped him to read between the lines and interpret situations as well as opportunities so as to leverage things in his favour. Right from the time he faced colour discrimination in South Africa at the age of twenty-four in 1893, till his death at the age of seventy-eight in 1948,

Gandhi was always on his feet, interacting with people and participating in eventful moments, some of which created history.

Gandhi's First Political Organization

After Gandhi tasted his first colour discrimination experience, within a year he formed the Natal Indian Congress to fight discrimination against Indians in South Africa. Natal is a region in South Africa whose main cities are Durban and Pietermaritzburg. This political organization was instrumental in introducing many petitions which were sent to the British rulers. Gandhi had that basic sense of creating an instant organization whenever it was required. He never shied away from taking initiative and mustering people for a cause. When the Boer War broke out in 1899, Gandhi was convinced that Indians must support the British troops in South Africa as their duty. He was also hopeful that such a gesture would build goodwill with the British rulers. He thus created an 'Indian Ambulance Corps' of around 1,100 men who would help wounded British soldiers. He himself participated in the war as a part of this contingent and was awarded the Queen's South Africa Medal for his service. He and the Corps worked as stretcher-bearers and expenses were met by the Indian community. Yet again Gandhi organized a small ambulance corps when the Zulu rebellion took place against the British. He again wanted to prove to the British that Indians in South Africa were there to help the British Empire. He captained a small group of twenty-one people to act as stretcher-bearers and helped the wounded.

Gandhi also established the *Indian Opinion* because he was convinced that without a vehicle for mass media it was impossible to sustain a movement against the British. With meagre funds he created a small organization and managed his own printing press. This newspaper was published in four languages.

Gandhi's First Taste of Community Living

Having been influenced by the Bhagwat Gita and John Ruskin's *Unto this Last*, Gandhi wanted to establish his own set-up where he could stay with volunteers and do some meaningful work as per his philosophy of Satyagraha and train his political activists and their families.

At Phoenix Settlement, a 100-acre farm, about 20 kilometres from Durban, Gandhi put into practice his community living, giving each family a two-acre piece of land to develop. It was like living in a large family which was self-sufficient and produced enough to meet its needs in areas such as food, cloth, grain, milk and milk products. Within a few years he turned it into a trust so that the establishment could run on its own for a long time. Gandhi even shifted his press and the newspaper to this farm so that it would be easy for him to monitor its progress.

People Power

Gandhi organized his first Satyagraha against the 'Black Act', a law which commanded Indians in South Africa to carry passes or identity cards all the time. Indians found it demeaning. Gandhi was arrested and put in jail with hundreds of his followers. People supported him in large numbers and several hundred passes were publicly burnt by many Indians. Gandhi learnt the important lesson that public demonstrations held peacefully yet innovatively could create an impact on law-keepers. He also learnt his first political lesson from this experience: if you lead fearlessly, people follow you.

Gandhi then started another community-living programme on a farm which was around 1,100 acres, near Johannesburg, donated by his German friend, Hermann Kallenbach. Here he organized a self-reliant lifestyle. He knew that those who supported him had to have the same livelihood. Initially an allowance was given on trust, and jail-going Satyagrahis were given an allowance according to what each family asked for. Gandhi realized very soon that this would not work for very long as there was room for fraud and also a resource constraint. If all families stayed in one place and worked together, then they could generate a 'cooperative common wealth'. Here Indians from different strata of society and different religions were to learn to live in harmony. On the farm were Hindus, Muslims, Christians and Parsis. Some of them ate meat, even beef. Gandhi took them into confidence and instead of making a rule for everyone to be vegetarian, he asked for their opinion. He could motivate every meat-eater to accept simple vegetarian food during their entire stay at the farm. Most of the construction work was undertaken by the members. They also learnt making sandals and the art of carpentry. He thus created a self-contained and self-sufficient organization.

Gandhi was a shrewd organizer and always backed the issues that affected the masses. He wanted his Satyagraha movement against the Brititsh to remain active and alive. In 1913 he, along with his comrades, opposed the British rule of not accepting Indian marriages as valid. As this 'andolan' or movement was not taking off well he focused simultaneously on another area of mass concern. It was a three-pound tax levied on Indian labour whose contract had expired (indenture expired Indians), for them to continue working. He managed to muster the Indians affected by this law and motivated them to go on a strike. He had the support of more than 4,000 coal miners, later rising to 10,000. But the British were not going to give up easily and started a crackdown on the ring leaders in order to break the strike.

Gandhi wanted to open another front as he was worried that the strike could lose its momentum. He was all set to have a 'padyatra' (march), to capture the government's attention. This was a daring idea and a brilliant concept which could deliver rich dividends. This was eventually referred to as 'the great march', where more than 2,000 people walked a distance of more than one hundred miles to court arrest. Gandhi got donations from Indians living in India. The cost of food and rations was almost 250 pounds a day and without these funds the march would have failed. Most of the participants were arrested and deported back to Natal, and Gandhi himself was sentenced to nine months' imprisonment with hard labour.

Establishing Sabarmati Ashram at Ahmedabad

Upon his return from South Africa, Gandhi wanted to establish an ashram in India. He had already obtained the experience of setting up ashrams or farms as mass dwelling units in South Africa. He chose Ahmedabad for three simple reasons. First, he was a Gujarati himself and was fluent with the language and aware of the culture. Second, he knew that Ahmedabad had many rich businessmen who would be able to contribute to his cause. Third, it was a centre for handloom and would help him establish a khadi industry as a part of the movement. He initially chose the Kochrab area of Ahmedabad and his first ashram in India was officially founded on 25 May 1915. It steadily developed as a centre for Gandhian studies to obtain self-sufficiency, practise Satyagraha and work for upliftment of the poor and take up the issue of untouchability.

Gandhi wanted to experiment with cow breeding, farming and khadi, handicraft and so, after a couple of years he moved to a piece of land on the banks of the Sabarmati River. He lived in this ashram until 1930, which later became the epicentre of the Indian freedom struggle. It was initially called Harijan Ashram, then the Satyagraha Ashram, and eventually it was known as Sabarmati Ashram. It was in this very place where Gandhi began his famous Salt March of 241 miles. In the middle of 1930 Gandhi decided to move out of the ashram, not to return until India acquired its independence. (He would never get a chance to return.)

Sabarmati Ashram was a thirty-six-acre barren piece of land which was later developed into a simple yet self-sufficient place where Satyagrahis lived and worked together as one large family—a family working together in search for the truth.

Fasts and Peaceful Strikes

From Sabarmati Ashram, which was his firm base, Gandhi conducted many peaceful protests and fasts to obtain justice for certain sections of people and, ultimately, to free India from the British.

He first fought for the ill-paid mill workers of Ahmedabad. The owners agreed to have discussions after Gandhi went on a three-day fast along with the mill workers, and the wages were suitably revised.

In March 1919 the British government passed a series of draconian laws against Indians to control public unrest, protests and conspiracy. This was known as the Rowlatt Act under the imposition of which political activists could be imprisoned up to two years without trial. Restrictions on the press, indefinite detention of the revolutionaries, arrests without warrants were the key points. Gandhi, along with other Indian leaders, went on an all-India strike marked with fasting and Satyagraha to protest against this act.

Under the same law, the infamous Jallianwala Bagh massacre was carried out in 1919. Following resistance by Indians, eventually in 1922, the British government repealed the act.

Organizing Impactful Events

Gandhi was extremely good at choosing the timing for his events. For example, to protest the Jallianwala Bagh massacre and Rowlatt Act, he began his 'non-cooperation movement' against the British Raj in 1920. The name of the movement was motivational in nature and simple enough for the masses to understand. It was supported by the Indian National Congress and the entire Indian public. The idea was to uphold Indian honour and dignity by adopting 'swadeshi' or locally made goods, refusing to buy British-made material of any sort. The response was overwhelming, with hundreds of thousands of people participating across the length and breadth of the country. By the summer of 1920 the British got worried that the movement should not become violent. Their fears proved true with the Chauri Chaura incident near Gorakhpur. Gandhi sensed the gravity of the situation immediately and gave a countrywide call to stop this movement in the middle of 1922. Still, he was imprisoned for six years.

One of the most significant and brilliantly crafted protests by Gandhi was the Salt March mentioned earlier. It was to mark protest against the salt tax, imposed by the British, which Gandhi considered unethical and against his fundamental rights. He started the march from Sabarmati Ashram on 12 March 1930 with just seventy-eight Satyagrahis. This was a well-thought out plan after Gandhi and Nehru, under the ageis of the Indian National Congress, declared 'Poorna Swaraj' or total independence from British Raj on 26 January 1930. The Congress thereafter gave complete charge to Gandhi to organize the first act of civil disobedience.

As a brilliant organizer, Gandhi made sure to be properly prepared for the march, which he wanted fully publicized. He started giving statements to the press a month in advance, thus giving even the foreign media enough time to make arrangements for covering the event. He made dramatic and emotionally appealing statements to the media such as, 'We are entering a life and death struggle and sacrifice. In this holy war we wish to offer ourselves as oblation.'

He ensured that he took only those with him who were trained Satyagrahis to minimize the chances of a breakout of violence. His twenty-four-day march over 241 miles crisscrossed forty-eight villages. He planned the entire journey very meticulously. The route and halts were selected on the basis of past contacts, recruiting potential, expected support and timing. Supporters and scouts were sent in advance to these villages to ensure that people knew when Gandhi would arrive at each stop and when he was he expected to give a talk. Most events were extensively covered by the local and foreign press. *The New York Times* wrote almost every day about the Salt March and Gandhi instantly became a household name abroad. The response was so huge that 100,000 people gathered around the first leg of the route. So many joined the march dressed in white khadi that the march was also dubbed as the 'white flowing river'.

Gandhi ended his yatra at Dandi village on 6 April, where he made 'illegal salt' by boiling salty mud in salty sea water. He said: 'With this action I am shaking the foundation of the British Empire.' He urged all Indians to make illegal salt wherever possible.

This triggered off a well-thought-out civil disobedience, which spread like wildfire as millions broke the Salt Law. By the end of the month, British authorities had arrested more than 60,000 people. What they failed to arrest was the fire that had already been started by Gandhi: the fire in the belly of all Indians wanting freedom.

Mass civil disobedience grew into mass Satyagraha: British goods were boycotted and people began defying British laws that were unpopular. This movement also saw many women joining the movement. Gandhi was arrested later in January 1932 and thrown in Yerwada Jail in Pune. Before his arrest he said, 'After my arrest I would ask the nation to wake up from its sleep.'

August Kranti or Quit India was yet another landmark movement led by Gandhi. Launched as massive civil disobedience in August 1942, it demanded an orderly but total withdrawal of Britishers from India. In a speech given in Bombay (now Mumbai) Gandhi gave an ultimatum: 'Do or die'. There, more than 60,000 protestors and supporters of Gandhi were arrested, many of them remaining in jail until the end of the Second World War. The Quit India movement was met with a heavy hand and the British pulled out all the stops in order to crush it. Most of the top Indian leaders were put in jail, and those who evaded arrest went underground. The British did not agree to leave India immediately but were prepared to consider it after the war was over.

Though this was Gandhi's last major movement, he kept up the resistance even after his wife's death. Despite his bad health he went on a twenty-one-day fast to demonstrate his resolve to oust the British. It was a trying time for Gandhi as most of the top Congress leaders were in jail and many nationalists had grown demoralized.

'I would like to see anyone, prophet, king or God, convince a thousand cats to do the same thing at the same time.'

—Neil Gaiman, author

LEADERSHIP LESSONS FROM A SAINT WITHOUT AUTHORITY

- Most of us work in organizations which have a defined structure and clear reporting roles. Each person has a defined job description, empowerment as per the designation and very clear guidelines and rules to follow. We have some standard operating procedures, some past data or records as well as documents to consult in our day's work. The first and perhaps most important lesson to learn from Gandhi is this: 'How do you make sense of chaos in situations and circumstances where there are no past precedents?' The second important learning is the ability to muster courage in an absolute alien environment. Both of these were evident from his South Africa experience where he was a nondescript young lawyer who had come to a foreign land to make a living.
- The ability to raise his voice against the powerful British rulers in a foreign land required a lot of guts. At the same time he was not even sure of the support of the Indian diaspora in South Africa, who were very small in number, to begin with. The community was neither organized nor motivated to fight. Moreover, most of the Indians were poor and had come to this foreign land to earn a living. Gandhi soon realized that in such circumstances that only a philosophy backed by total selfless commitment could possibly bring some results.
- Gandhi taught the world that if you have a vision, people will support you. In addition, taking initiative always reaps its benefits. Do not wait for

someone to tell you what to do; seize the moment and go for it. If thereafter you have the will to pursue your objectives, things will definitely work out in your favour.
- He also taught us to come up with our own original solutions and organizational models. He created self-contained and self-sufficient organizations, where everything was created and produced within. He made sure to involve each and every member of the organization and strove to motivate them all. His ashrams worked on this philosophy. In modern organizations too we should strive to involve everyone and create zero dependency on outside resources, as far as possible, especially for critical needs.
- Gandhi also taught us to take up issues that have mass support. Therefore, either support an issue that is popular or make your issue popular enough to garner support. In corporate or management parlance one calls it a 'buy in' where people buy into a project, concept or an idea led or initiated by you.
- Another important strategy that Gandhi followed was to keep the hearth hot. If one approach was not sufficient, he opened another front and ensured that the tempo was always maintained. He had his hand on the pulse of the people. Such keen social intelligence is very important for a leadership role: a leader must have his ear to the ground at all times and understand the pain points of his people.
- Gandhi also taught us how to organize events, plan complex yatras, involve and inform the press to get the maximum mileage possible. He had a great sense of timing, which every leader must have.

8

SELF-DISCIPLINE AND SELF-CONDUCT

Saint and Soldier

'Self-denial and self-discipline, however, will be recognized as the outstanding qualities of a good soldier.'

—William Lyon Mackenzie King,
Canadian political leader during the 1920s to 1940s

To be successful as a leader—or even as an 'ordinary' individual who is not a leader—two things are most important: self-discipline and self-conduct. Many people are lucky that they are inherently disciplined, gifted by God and their upbringing with such a trait. Most others who are not naturally endowed with such virtues have to make a conscious effort to develop them. All of us are influenced by our upbringing and learn to be disciplined because of our teachers, schooling and parents.

In his childhood, Gandhi did not display any extraordinary traits of being highly disciplined or possessing a strong willpower. He was like any other normal young boy, though he remained within the prescribed limits of behaviour because of his father, who was very strict regarding discipline and the behaviour of his children. Gandhi was not a rebellious child; on the contrary he was quite obedient.

Awareness or awakening brings responsibility and, in turn, responsibility triggers discipline. Something similar happened with Mahatma Gandhi, who was not born a 'Mahatma' but gradually transformed himself into a living legend by his karma and strict self-control. Gandhi's turning point was his move from Bombay to South Africa, which was to become his learning ground for almost a decade. Other than the incident when he was thrown out of a first-class compartment of a train for being non-white, he was also a witness to the everyday harassment and humiliation that all Indians working in South Africa were being subjected to. It was this that finally made him act against racial discrimination. Once he had decided that he would not tolerate discrimination and would take up the responsibility to eradicate this injustice, he quickly transformed into a very serious responsible leader of all Indians living in South Africa.

I feel the enormity of the task at hand and the apparent might of the British made him realize that without concerted effort backed by dedication and discipline, he would not be able to accomplish his mission. It was his belief and strong resolve that set him on a course of sacrifice, self-control and self-discipline. This spirit is demonstrated by his statement, 'If I have the belief that I can do it, I shall surely acquire the capacity to do it even if I may not have it at the beginning.'

Discipline and Sense of Responsibility at All Times

Every aspect of Gandhi's philosophy required discipline and courage for it to spell success. He had chosen a difficult path to achieve his mission, therefore he had to demonstrate to his followers that not only did he mean what he said, but more importantly, he practised what he preached.

The Phoenix and Tolstoy farms were established by Mahatma Gandhi in South Africa to inculcate a sense of discipline, hard work, and simplicity in all Satyagrahis. By spending each of his days with purpose and according to a strict timetable, he was able to create a vibrant culture which had a very positive impact on each one of the inmates of these ashrams. He was a firm believer in what Krishnamachari said: 'No one is wise by birth. Wisdom results from one's own efforts.'

A Disciplined Life of a Saint and a Soldier

As a leader who always walked the talk, Gandhi demonstrated certain traits which became synonymous with him and his name. One of the major reasons for his success and that of his movement was his self-discipline and strong willpower.

Punctuality

Out of all the things that Gandhi bought during his stay in England as a law student, the only thing that he retained from among his so-called gentleman's attire was his watch, which always hung down the left of his waist. That watch was like a meter that regulated his life; he considered his watch to be his best and most useful possession, so much so that he sent a pocket watch each as gifts to the two detectives in London who were attached to him during his visit in 1931, with an inscription, 'With love from M.K. Gandhi.'

Gandhi was a stickler for punctuality and even Lokmanya Tilak, the social reformer and popular leader of the freedom struggle, was ticked off by him when he reached half an hour late for a conference at Godhra in Gujarat. Gandhi said, 'If we get our Swaraj half an hour late, then the blame will go to Lokmanyaji.'

Nirmal Kumar Bose, an educationist who was an activist for the freedom struggle with Gandhi, recalled that people assisting Gandhi had to ensure that his alarm was set on the pocket watch at 4 a.m. and all the things that he needed, including his toothbrush, were kept in appropriate places next to his bed because he did not want to waste even a minute in looking for them.

Gandhi, unfortunately, failed to check his watch a few minutes before he was assassinated. His prayer meeting was to start at 5 p.m. and at 4.55 his assistant, Abha, told him, 'Bapu, your pocket watch must be feeling neglected today as you did not even look at it.'

Sri Sri Ravi Shankar's guru, Pandit Sudhakar Chaturvedi, was also a Gandhian who not only taught Gandhi about the Vedas but also took down dictation for letters that the Mahatma had to write to important people. Once while travelling to Darjeeling in a train he was taking dictation, when the guard accidently disconnected the last three bogies and there was commotion in the compartment. Amidst all the panic Gandhi continued dictating to him. The pandit said, 'We are in between life and death, we may not even live.' Gandhi replied, 'If we get saved, we would have wasted all that time. But if we die, we die; so come on, take the dictation and do not waste time.'

Austerity

Gandhi was against wasting anything, whether food, cloth, or money. For him, the practise of austerity was a spiritual goal. His personal requirements were minimal and for his own comforts he had no demands.

Gandhi was prepared to cook his own food and regularly lent a helping hand in the kitchen in all his ashrams. He would feed the animals and look after the sick ones himself. While in Yerwada jail, the jail superintendent looked at Gandhi as an honoured guest and laid out lavish furniture and crockery for him to use. Gandhi refused all that and lived with a plate and a tumbler insisting that not more than Rs. 35 per month should be spent on him as against the official budget of Rs. 150. Gandhi cleaned his own toilet and encouraged everyone in the ashram to do the same.

His whole philosophy was not to waste resources, which was reflected in his message: 'There is enough for everybody's need, but not for everybody's greed.'

Control of Palate

Gandhi was against over-indulgence. He proposed and practised frugalism in eating habits. He was of the opinion that parents, out of false affection, give their children a variety of foods which are bad for the health. 'We should not think of food all the twenty-four hours of the day but eat only limited meals which cater to the needs of our body.' He looked at food as a medicine and not as a means of pleasure. He therefore abstained from spicy condiments and was a pure vegetarian. To develop strong willpower, he felt that the control of the palate was a valuable aid for the control of the mind.

Unclothing of the Mahatma

To give up good clothes is a big sacrifice. And sacrifice requires disciplined motivation. The sartorial audacity of Gandhi was no mean achievement. How many of us can resist branded clothes and accessories when we enter a mall, for instance? Only a strong disciplined mind can stop you from pulling out and swiping a credit card to buy a nice pair of shoes! Gandhi disciplined himself to control the temptation to purchase anything material which he considered in excess of his needs.

He spent time on his charkha to spin his own yarn, which later became a national symbol of self-reliance.

Discipline in Practising Non-violence

It is easy to lead a mob in a frenzy to inflict injury to others, but it requires a lot of patience and self-control to lead people to protest peacefully and remain so even in the face of provocation. Gandhi's self-discipline, which he wore on his sleeve, was the greatest contributing factor for the success of his non-violence movement. The idea of living on a farm was to build a collective conscience amongst his followers. It was a highly disciplined life which they lived collectively that was coming handy to fight the mighty British Empire.

The infamous massacre at Jallianwala Bagh, where hundreds of innocent Indians were killed, is a case in point. It started with an incident which many will not know. Two days before the massacre in Amritsar on 11 April 1919, an English lady, Marcella Sherwood, was apprehended by a mob of Indians and beaten very badly. Local British commander, General Dyer, was furious and issued orders requiring every Indian using that street to crawl on his hands and knees. He said: 'I want them to know that a British woman is as sacred as a Hindu god and therefore they have to crawl in front of her too!' He also ordered the public whipping of locals who even came close to a British policeman. The atmosphere was therefore very charged with anger on both sides. When Dyer learnt that Indians were protesting in Jallianwala Bagh while celebrating the Baisakhi festival on 13 April, he and his men opened fire at the crowd, killing nearly 400 men, women, and children.

Mahatma Gandhi had to demonstrate patience and resilience to overcome this shock. In protest of the mass killing, he returned the Kaiser-i-Hind medal given to him for his work during the Boer War. Like him, Rabindranath Tagore, the great Bengali poet and playwright, protested too by renouncing his knighthood. Yet despite such harsh action by the British, Gandhi remained committed to his non-violent philosophy.

To Be Ethical Requires Willpower

'Strength does not come from physical capacity. It comes from an indomitable will'. Thus said Mahatma Gandhi. To be ethical requires not only a deep conviction but also a strong willpower. People who have to live by their principles have to pay a heavy price: sacrifice, the ability to take humiliation, and determination to stay on course. For Gandhi it was like being the captain of a ship in the middle of a storm, who had to take it to the shore without even a compass! He was in absolutely unchartered waters and had to rely only on his willpower and his inner conscience. It requires a lot of courage. As Winston Churchill put it: 'Success is not final, failure is not fatal; it is the courage to continue that counts.'

A son tells the story of his eighty-eight-year-old mother who suffered a fall and had to be hospitalized. As a family, seeing her condition after the accident, they were not sure if she would pull through. But the old lady had the most remarkable will to survive and eventually after a long hospital stay, she did recover, almost fully. As Benjamin Disraeli said, 'Nothing can withstand the power of the human will if it is willing to stake its very existence to the extent of its purpose.'

Fast for Self-control

Fasting was a weapon which Gandhi used as a part of his philosophy of Ahinsa or non-violence. He was also of the opinion that fasting builds resilience and self-control. If one examines them, most religions encourage fasting in some form or the other. The idea is to practise self-denial so that one becomes spiritually strong and does not fall prey to temptations. Fasting teaches you to say no.

Mahatma Gandhi fasted seventeen times in the course of India's freedom movement. The longest fast he undertook was in Delhi in 1943, for twenty-one days. Eventually he perfected his routine for fasting. He started his fast with lemon juice and honey. He only drank salted lemon juice throughout the day and slept long hours to preserve his energy. People usually fast on fruits but Gandhi's fast was total, and he came out of each fast safe and sound.

Fasting is like punishing oneself for a cause and it requires a tremendous sense of self-sacrifice.

Detachment and Non-possession

Gandhi welcomed people from all religions, castes and of all skin colours, to stay in his ashrams. He looked at religion as a way of living and expected all inmates to follow simple rules that were applicable to all. He used to say, 'Whoever joins me must be ready to sleep on the plain floor, wear simple clothes, get up early, live on undemanding nutrition and even clean his own toilet.'

Gandhi was inspired by the ancient idea of a hermitage where humans and animals could co-exist, making use of natural surroundings. His ashrams had everything required to live a simple life. Though living was hard—everybody had to do their bit of cleaning, handling the flour machines, drawing water, washing clothes, doing kitchen work. They had their own tailoring shop where simple clothes could be stitched and repaired for those staying in the ashram. It worked with the clockwork-precision of a military garrison but with the heart and spirit of a temple.

Bread Labour

Gandhi always supported dignity of labour. He was impressed by the writings of Leo Tolstoy, who emphasized that every human being should work to earn his bread and this work had to be hard manual work. It was based on the laws of the Bible which said: 'God created man to work for food and said that those who ate without work were thieves.' Nature intended that we earn our bread by the sweat of our brow. Gandhi said it was after he read Tolstoy that he started to believe in the natural law that man must work for his food. He also knew that the Gita spoke of the same theme.

Even a rich man would get tired of rest and comfort and fall sick if he always ate without exercising at all. And that is why one has to exercise in some form or the other. Then why should we not engage in some exercise which yields productivity at the same time? This is exactly what the concept of bread labour is. Church service, 'seva' in Gurudwara or 'shram daan' in a temple, are all different forms of labour.

A God-like Stance: Celibacy

Gandhi was known to have very few 'worldly possessions'. He gradually realized the importance of 'brahamacharya', or self-imposed celibacy, which according to the Hindu scriptures is an essential requirement for spiritual practice. Even in other religions, nuns and monks, for instance, need to abstain from sex and remain celibate in body and mind.

Gandhi believed that brahamacharya, like all other disciplines, must be observed not only in deed but also in thought and word. 'Life without brahmacharya appears to me to be insipid and animal-like,' he said.

Though married, Gandhi practised celibacy from the age of thirty-five until his death more than forty years later. He believed that 'Man is a man because he is capable of distinguishing a wife, mother, sister and a daughter'. He believed, as written in scriptures, that it requires immense willpower to practise brahmacharya, which also thereafter helps build restraint and sense of sacrifice.

Self-discipline Should Be Contagious

The basic purpose of a leader wearing his self-discipline on his sleeve is to motivate all those who are around him to embrace the same. Since Gandhi was leading millions of Indians to fight for freedom, it was very important for him to discipline his followers. He achieved this by practising what he preached. He made a strict code of conduct for himself and by staying on the ashrams in South Africa and in India along with his followers, he could influence them positively to adopt his good qualities, especially those related to discipline and simplicity.

Importance of Self-discipline

Self-control, delayed gratification, sacrifice and discipline, are probably the most important tenents of emotional intelligence. If one looks at successful people, regardless of their profession, one would identify in them a strong sense of self-discipline.

Looking at successful personalities in the movie industry, for example Amitabh Bachchan, Shahrukh Khan, Lata Mangeshkar or Farhan Akhtar, one would find a strong sense of responsibility and self-discipline, coupled with the ability to work very hard tirelessly day on day throughout their long careers. While the lives of film stars may look glamorous, one should not discount the dedication and hard work which they have had to nurture over the years.

Sportspersons also have to work extremely hard, control their diet, heed the advice of their coaches, and follow strict regimens prescribed by experts. Sachin Tendulkar, Mohammad Ali, Milkha Singh or Andre Agassi, for example—all demonstrated a high level of commitment and dedication. Tennis great Andre Agassi recently tweeted: 'Nothing can substitute for just plain hard work. I had to put in the time to get back. It was a grind. It meant sweating every day but I was completely committed.'

Looking at successful business leaders and entrepreneurs across the world, all of them without exception demonstrated hard work, self-discipline and willpower to succeed. Pick up names like Ratan Tata, Azim Premji or former CEO of General Electric, Jack Welch and you will find this to be true.

'In the absence of willpower the most complete collection of virtues and talents is wholly worthless.'
—Aleister Crowley, English occultist,
painter, poet and novelist

SELF-DISCIPLINE AND SELF-CONDUCT

> **LEADERSHIP LESSONS FROM A SAINT WITHOUT AUTHORITY**
>
> - You cannot accomplish anything big in life without discipline and sacrifice. This is required for every profession, every mission and for any vision to be accomplished.
> - Discipline can be inculcated in your team, your subordinates or even in your family only if you yourself are disciplined.
> - One requires very strong willpower in order to lead a simple life, especially when you have the means to splurge and live an ostentatious lifestyle.
> - One must do physical effort in a day's work. It would be great to view it as 'Bread Labour'. People who lead a sedentary life would benefit greatly from this practice. It not only helps in keeping physically fit but also gives one mental satisfaction.
> - One should be able to lead by example and lay down common ground rules for all the people in an organization, regardless of position or designation.

9

GANDHI'S CHARISMA

Something that Money Can't Buy

'Always be yourself, express yourself, have faith in yourself, do not go out and look for a successful personality and duplicate it.'
—Bruce Lee, Chinese-American martial artist,
actor and filmmaker

What Is Charisma?

Are people born with charisma or is it a characteristic that develops over time? This is an often debatable topic in the leadership continuum. In practice, though, it is clear that some people have charisma as a natural gift and then there are those who develop it over time.

In simple words, charismatic individuals are those who have a so-called 'magnetic' personality. People are drawn to them, for reasons which may be hard to explain; people simply get attracted to them, look up to them and feel reassured in their very presence.

For instance, Winston Churchill, Adolf Hitler, Franklin D. Roosevelt, Harry Truman, Indira Gandhi and Abraham Lincoln were all iconic personalities in the political space who left a huge impact not only on their immediate subordinates but also the world at large.

Spiritual leaders like Vivekanand, Gautam Buddha and Mother Teresa also had a halo around them. Among contemporary corporate leaders, Richard Branson, J.R.D. Tata, the late Steve Jobs and Jack Welch all had that certain panache about them.

Actors like Amitabh Bachchan, Al Pacino, Richard Burton, Meryl Streep, Leonardo DiCaprio, Clint Eastwood and Morgan Freeman have a charismatic screen presence. They occupy the whole screen even with other actors in the same frame.

There is something about these people that cannot be exactly described. One can call it panache, pizzazz, or allure. One might say they are simply fascinating. *'Je ne sais quoi',* or 'I know not what', is how the French language defines it.

Similarly, Gandhi was an enigma or a kaleidoscopic personality, which meant different things to different people. To some he appeared to be a martyr, an evangelist, revolutionary and patriot. The Western world looked at him as a fanatic, a saint or a charlatan while some called him a misguided politician, a maverick or even a political quack.

A frail man who at a first glance could pass off as a nondescript, ordinary Indian was to influence millions not only during his lifetime but also even sixty years after his death. Despite the seeming ordinariness of his appearance, he had a persona which was nothing short of charismatic. People from all walks of life, the poor, the beggars, the kings and queens, the intellectual and the ordinary—everyone was in awe of this man.

It is said that when people met Winston Churchill, they felt they could do anything whereas Hitler made people feel that 'only he' could fulfil their aspirations. In Gandhi's case it was very different. He could motivate people to do things collectively and make them feel, 'Yes, we can do it together.' People relate enigmatic personalities to oratory skills, stage presence, authority or even style and sophistication. But Gandhi had none of these. His simplicity, his hardcore humane approach of non-violence and his philosophy were possibly most responsible for his charisma.

Charisma and Success

It is a classic chicken-and-egg question: do people with charisma become successful or do successful people acquire their charisma?

In the case of Gandhi, he was a thin, short child who showed no signs of being extraordinary in any way. As a practising lawyer, in his very first case he could not think of a single question as he stood before the judge and had to hand over the case to a colleague. After that, he did not get another case.

Gandhi had no authority, no title and was not even a great speaker. It was his hard work, dedication and perseverance which brought him success after a long struggle. His passion made him a hero. Due to his commitment to fight for his cause he could address a public meeting effectively. Gradually he could influence people and invoke belief in them. Once he was successful in influencing people, they started to think of him as a charismatic person.

Adolf Hitler similarly was a nondescript corporal during the First World War. During his first few public appearances, he did make an impact on his small audience, but eventually he grew in stature and managed to have an aura around him only after he acquired considerable political power.

In the twentieth century a business leader was expected to have charisma before he came on the scene. Examples are aplenty: Robert McNamara, US secretary of defense; or Lee Iacocca, head of Chrysler corporation, who had awesome and towering personalities and possibly became successful because they were already influential, overpowering and charismatic. In recent times the late Steve Jobs's charisma came into being because of his achievements at Apple.

For modern management, this has wider implications. Today, a leader is not only an influencer but has to first be an enabler or a doer. He has to lead from the front; he has to be a part of the team all the time.

I feel that Gandhi, who surfaced in the beginning of the twentieth century, is an example of modern leadership and of a charismatic manager who survives by example. With flat organizations and lesser hierarchy, the Gandhian style of functioning would be better suited for modern management scenarios.

Gandhi's Contribution to Modern Management

Gandhi gave to modern management some very concrete concepts. For one, he proved by demonstrating that self-actualization through self-motivation is essential for being an awe-inspiring leader. A leader must get inspired by the environment—in his case, the social scenario—in order to take up the challenge. He not only attained self-actualization himself but inspired his followers to move to that level.

He also proved that charismatic leaders do not seek conventional power; rather, they look for social power and want their followers to revere them and see them as their saviours. In that context even Hitler and his cronies projected themselves as messiahs for the Germans after they lost the First World War. But Hitler soon became power-hungry and declared himself as the Fuhrer of the German state.

Gandhi also demonstrated that great leaders have a self-correcting nature. They are their own greatest critics and continually strive to become better. They are aware that this superiority or goodness in them makes them different from the masses. And when their followers reach their level of goodness, they themselves move a notch higher. They always maintain such a gap between themselves and their followers.

Moreover, Gandhi left behind a great idea of creating a 'leadership philosophy'. Volumes of research continue to be devoted to the study of Gandhian philosophy. Followers of this philosophy are called 'Gandhians'. It almost comes close to being a cult or a sect, as a number of people have embraced the philosophy even after the Mahatma departed from this world.

Gandhi's Lessons in Developing a Towering Personality

Hundreds of biographies have been written on Gandhi. Pandit Jawaharlal Nehru once wrote: 'No man can write a real life of Gandhi, unless he is as big as Gandhi.' He went on to say, 'He invested many gestures with symbolic meaning so that there exists not one Gandhi, but hundreds of Gandhis.'

Modern leaders must understand that to become a charismatic leader, one has to first achieve a certain level of success through hard work and dedication. Gandhi certainly did so. The second important learning is that dedication is possible only if a leader is passionate about his purpose.

The most important lesson from Gandhi is that to be a

charismatic personality one need not have an overwhelming physical appearance. Your sense of purpose must be 'demonstratable' and infectious to an extent.

'Charisma is the result of effective leadership, not the other way around.'

—Warren Bennis and Burt Nanus, authors of the book
Leaders: Strategies for Taking Charge

LEADERSHIP LESSONS FROM A SAINT WITHOUT AUTHORITY

- If you are not born with a charismatic personality, you can develop it over time.
- Charisma has more to do with your intentions, abilities and passion. You need to demonstrate it to your subordinates.
- You need not be a great orator or have a towering personality to be charismatic.
- Though good attire helps in creating a good impression on your audience, ultimately it is your sincerity of purpose and your ability to think out of the box that will make people look up to you.
- You should strive to achieve your goals, slowly and steadily backed with hard work and dedication. Charisma will follow.

10

COLLABORATIVE SUCCESS

Role of a Spouse in a Leader's Life

'Many marriages would be better if the husband and the wife clearly understood that they are on the same side.'
—Zig Ziglar, American author and motivational speaker

'Behind every successful man there is a great woman'. This famous saying is perfectly true for Mahatma Gandhi, for whom his wife Kasturba Gandhi was a pillar of support, right from his initial days as an ordinary lawyer right up to his tumultuous years as a leader of a freedom movement.

Kasturba Gandhi got married to Mohandas Karamchand Gandhi at a very young age, in 1883, when they were only thirteen years old. Kasturba, who came from a well-to-do business family, was six months older than her husband. She was barely literate but had a mind of her own; it was not easy for her husband to force his decisions on her. As Mahatma Gandhi once told John S. Hoyland, an author: 'I learnt the lesson of non-violence from my wife when I tried to bend her will to my ways. Her resistance to my will and her quiet non-violent submission to my stupid ways ultimately made me ashamed of my stupidity and my belief that I was born to rule over her. Ultimately she was my teacher for practising non-violence.' Though there was a huge intellectual gap between the two, Gandhi gradually learnt to respect his wife's ideas and opinions.

People who are very successful in life always need the support of their spouses, be it emotional or physical. If the spouse also becomes equally ambitious and wants to outdo the partner, as is the case with contemporary couples, then the marital relationship can develop serious cracks. In the realm of leadership, each must understand the importance of the other's role, responsibilities and should play a supportive role to make 'their life' successful. It has to be a collaborative success. It does not mean that either is being dumped or relegated to the lower rung of the ladder. It is more to do with one's attitude. Look at the first lady of the United States of America. While the husband performs the duties of a president, the lady has more than enough on her hands to contribute independently. In the case of Bill Clinton, his wife Hillary performed the duties of the first lady perfectly, played her role effectively and made her presence felt as long as it was required. After her husband's tenure was over, she joined active politics and ran for the presidency as well. Later she was appointed secretary of state in Barack Obama's government.

Gandhi lived in different times, when wives of Indian political leaders were not at all in prominence. Look at Ambedkar, for example, or Patel, Bose, Nehru, Tilak and Tagore: their spouses do not figure much in the limelight. Wives of the old days were expected to be out of sight; women were confined to their homes.

Kasturba Gandhi was an exception. She stood shoulder to

shoulder with her husband. She went to jail for his cause, which was hers as well. She actively took part in public campaigns, about which Gandhi wrote and spoke often. A wife cannot and should not be taken for granted by her husband, but Gandhi did impose some of his radical ideas on Kasturba. Shunning untouchability, cleaning one's own toilet and accepting celibacy—these were some of the ideas that Gandhi was very passionate about.

As Kasturba realized the importance of her husband's task, she became convinced and accepted what came her way.

Arun Manilal Gandhi, grandson of the Mahatma, once very aptly said, 'While Gandhi experimented with truth, Kasturba experienced it.' But Gandhi had to reason with his wife and once she was convinced, she would fully support him. This was the first lesson Gandhi learnt in Satyagraha: that one has to convince others by reason and not force. A companion doesn't have to have degrees, but needs to have basic common sense and a strong sense to differentiate between what is right and what is wrong. Moreover, a spouse must have the ability to point out if his or her partner is going wrong while making any decisions. Wives with a sound mind can be the greatest asset for their husbands. As their relationship matured it was difficult to imagine Gandhi without Kasturba.

A True Better Half

As a wife, the centre of Kasturba's thoughts was always Gandhi. She once said, 'My religion is my husband.' Gandhi, for his part, said, 'Kasturba has lost herself in me and is my true better half.'

Kasturba was a pillar of Gandhian thought in every possible

way. Without her support and sacrifice, Gandhi may not have been able to achieve what he did in his lifetime. She sacrificed all her likes, customs and comforts and also gave up prejudices like untouchability and casteism. She also had to go through a number of long separations as her husband travelled often, first for studies and later to work abroad. Eventually, his political life made him travel even more frequently. They were also jailed separately several times. Wherever she went along with him, she made a house into a home by her strong commitment and mere presence.

Though they had their share of arguments and disagreements in private, she stood behind him all throughout his struggle for the people of India. She remained mostly in the background but Gandhi knew that she was there to always give him support.

Political Life and Contributions

Kasturba Gandhi infused new blood into India's women by inspiring them to metamorphose from housewives to political workers.

She herself was jailed several times and encouraged women to come forward for the freedom struggle.

Price of Political Activism

Mahatma Gandhi knew that women could help bring about a paradigm shift in Satyagraha. He also knew that it would be difficult for the British to use force on women, especially when they were unarmed. He realized that women had a stronger constitution and a stout heart that one requires for peaceful agitation. He was not sure if Kasturba would actively participate in agitation and did not want to push her into it. However his wife had made up her mind to join the freedom fight and was ready to face the consequences. When Gandhi discouraged her, she said, 'I also want to take the path to which you are inviting others. What do I lack that disqualifies me to go to jail?' She was the one who illegally crossed the Transvaal border in South Africa in September 1913, along with fifteen others, in disobedience of the British law; they were arrested and sentenced to three months' imprisonment with hard labour. During her time in prison she motivated other women to find courage to survive the difficult and harsh routine.

Message of Self-sufficiency

Kasturba complemented her husband's efforts wholeheartedly. Once she returned to India, she assumed the charge of reaching out to the women and organizing them as an effective outfit. Gandhi started his first campaign over the conditions of farmers in Champaran, Bihar. Kasturba gathered the women of that area, taught them to be self-sufficient and to give importance to hygiene and sanitation. Later, in Sabarmati Ashram, she learnt how to use the charkha and propagated the spinning-and-weaving drive of self-sufficiency for women across the country.

Social Service

Kasturba's keen instinct made her reach out to people in need. In 1904 in South Africa, there was a bubonic plague epidemic in Johannesburg. Kasturba reached out to the Indian community and educated them on the importance of hygiene in such circumstances and how to detect warning signs of an onset of plague.

Kasturba's Life on the Farms of South Africa

Mahatma Gandhi established his first ashram called Phoenix settlement in Durban, South Africa, in 1904. Kasturba Gandhi made this her home for a long time and led many Satyagraha activities from there. In 1913 she protested against discriminatory working conditions for Indians from this farm and courted arrest.

Phoenix settlement was a place far from civilization, where the nearest connectivity point was a railway station two miles away. Her husband was mostly at Johannesburg staying at Tolstoy Farm, which was the second such tenement established for their movement. Gandhi had to spend more time at Johannesburg as the movement was better controlled from there. When Gandhi was arrested in 1908 and imprisoned for two months, Kasturba decided to eat the same food that her husband got in the prison. As it was not possible for her to share the hardships of a jail then, she found such ways to show her solidarity. Whenever Gandhi was away from the Phoenix settlement, Kasturba took charge as the matriarch and saw to the needs of all residents.

Kasturba's biggest agony was that her sons were also taking part in the agitation. There was a conflict between her allegiance to her husband and her love and duty to her children. Her son Harilal Gandhi wanted to become a barrister and sought to go to England for higher studies. His father was against it, because it would have gone against their struggle against the British. Rebelling against this decision, Harilal broke ties with his family in 1911 and left South Africa. It was a big jolt to Kasturba as a mother, but she continued supporting her husband even after this.

Sabarmati Ashram at Gujarat

Once they reached India in 1915, Gandhi and Kasturba realized that they needed a big place to accommodate all the people involved with their movement. They had had enough experience of establishing a large farm for such a purpose in South Africa. Kasturba looked after the Sabarmati Ashram and except while she travelled with him, she ensured personally that the ashram operated with clockwork precision. It is here that she picked up the art of using the charkha. She implored women to become 'quiet revolutionaries' by using charkha and wearing hand-spun khadi, a symbol of self-reliance.

In 1930, as the movement against the British became more intense, a large number of men were imprisoned. Kasturba realized that now was the time to involve more and more women. Therefore she left the running of Sabarmati Ashram to other ladies and started her travels, urging more women to join the movement. In 1931, with Sabarmati as her base, she accompanied her husband to meet Viceroy Lord Irwin in Shimla to discuss the end of the civil disobedience movement. However, when Gandhi went to London to attend a round-table conference, Kasturba refused to join him as she felt she had enough to do back home.

Kasturba was also instrumental in raising funds for the Indian freedom movement. Indian women from abroad, especially South Africans, donated money for this cause. In September 1932 Gandhi went on a fast unto death to oppose the newly proposed Constitution which would establish a separate electorate for untouchables. His wife took active part in the fight against untouchability and toured southern India to plead for Harijans. From 1932 to the next two years, Kasturba was arrested and jailed several times, the longest sentence being six months in Sabarmati Jail. The British started feeling that she was as big a threat to law and order as her husband and to prevent her from influencing other women inmates she was locked up in a separate room.

Since the ashram was the epicentre of India's freedom movement, the British government decided to seize it. The ashram was deserted as most of the men and women participating in the freedom movement had been arrested. Gandhi decided to disband the ashram in 1933.

Gandhi and Kasturba moved to Bombay due to his ill health. Later in 1936 they started Sevagram, a small ashram in Wardha. These were tough years for Kasturba who realized that her son Harilal had started drinking heavily and was publicly criticizing his father. It was a big embarrassment for both husband and wife who were considered saints by the entire country.

In 1942, with Gandhi at the helm, the 'Quit India' movement was born. In the month of August Gandhi was arrested, and Kasturba thereafter addressed a political meeting in Mumbai where she was also arrested. Both were lodged in the Aga Khan Palace at Pune.

Aga Khan Palace

It is at this palace that Mahatma Gandhi went on a twenty-one-day fast. Here, Kasturba supported her husband by limiting her diet to the minimum, even as her health was failing, causing Gandhi grave concern. The palace became a hub for political activity as people often came to see Gandhi.

At the palace, Kasturba died aged seventy-four on 22 February 1944.

Kasturba led a tough life, fighting for Indians alongside her husband. Frequent jail sentences, poor diet and her health issues made her very weak and resulted in diminishing health.

Though Kasturba lived a life based on her husband's principles of simplicity, celibacy and bread-labour, she had her own moments of joy and satisfaction. She and her husband enjoyed the people's complete loyalty and the entire nation respected them. They were objects of reverence.

Yet Kasturba demonstrated an equanimous mind and never let the power and praise go to her head. She maintained the decorum and sanctity of the place she lived in and the forums she represented.

A Husband's Wife; a Wife's Husband

Mahatma Gandhi found a fully supportive life partner in his wife. When a spouse has to play a role effectively, he or she needs the complete and unconditional support of their partner. If one comes to think of it, marriage itself is a pledge for an 'unconditional bond' for both life partners.

One would have realized by now that Gandhi would not have been able to achieve what he did without Kasturba. She was like his shadow. Your shadow can be in front or on the side or at the back depending on the position of the sun. Therefore your partner could be sometimes leading you, sometimes following you and sometimes just being next to you. But she is with you for certain.

In today's context when there is a lot of stress on women's empowerment, this aspect becomes very relevant. A shadow can be alongside you and not necessarily behind you. Kasturba, most of the time, managed to do whatever she wanted to do; she had her own mind and own action plan. But, at the end of the day, she was aligned with the freedom movement and her husband's philosophy.

Contemporary managers, CEOs and entrepreneurs do require the support of their spouses. It is for the spouse to understand the problems and challenges that their partners face at work. Mutual consultation is very important. This requires personality match more than an educational match between the two. Kasturba, for example, was barely literate but she was as worldly wise as her husband.

> *'By all means, marry. If you get a good wife, you'll become happy; if you get a bad one, you'll become a philosopher.'*
> —Socrates, Greek philosopher

LEADERSHIP LESSONS FROM A SAINT WITHOUT AUTHORITY

- To be successful one must have a supportive spouse.
- There has to be a great understanding between husband and wife for a successful, eventful life.
- Husbands and wives need to be mutually supportive and should take interest in each other's work.
- A cooperative spouse can also be, at the same time, a constructive critic of their partner's work.
- Women do tend to have keen common sense and men must draw upon this strength. Wisdom does not come with degrees; it has other manifestations.
- Women often are emotionally stronger than men and can be a great emotional support.
- One has to be lucky to have a supportive spouse who believes in 'collaborative success' for both as one entity.

11

SPIRITUALIZATION OF POLITICS

Benevolent Leadership, a Paradigm Shift

'For peace is not mere absence of war, but is a virtue that springs from, a state of mind, a disposition for benevolence, confidence, and justice.'
—Baruch Spinoza, Dutch philosopher

Power of Faith and Defining Spirituality

'Spirituality' may be one of the most used words in the world but it has no universally accepted definition. The concept, for many, is an illusion; for some it's like a mirage. It is usually understood as faith, love, compassion, enlightenment, higher consciousness, cosmic, divine, a higher power and even self-actualization. In the most basic form it has goodness of the heart and community as well as mankind at its centre. This can be looked as 'applied spirituality'. It is a commitment to live by a code of conduct that is in line with your inner self, which usually translates to responsibility towards the world we live in. This threads through all religions.

One may not be able to specifically define spirituality; yet the fact is that faith has immense power over its followers, to the extent that it can motivate people to give their life for something so abstract.

The United Nations Educational, Scientific and Cultural Organization (UNESCO) has been able to realize the power of faith and spirituality for bringing peace across our planet, which is reflected in their Constitution. It reads: 'Since wars begin in the minds of men, it is in the minds of men that the defense of peace must be constructed.' It directly points at bringing about an inner change in our top leadership, business or otherwise. It would be prudent to point out that most wars take place for materialistic gains, which create an impact on business. Conversely, in several cases, in order to have brisk business wars are declared. Nations wage war for oil and natural resources, businessmen want wars in order to sell arms and other wares required to support them.

Gandhi's Concept of 'Spiritualization of Politics'

Mahatma Gandhi was probably the first leader who followed a unique humanitarian approach to leadership. After all, leadership is usually related to power, control, privilege and money. Leaders contemporary to Gandhi like Mussolini, Stalin, Hitler, Churchill and Roosevelt, were all for power and control.

Gandhian philosophy, meanwhile, is driven by compassion, service for others and non-violence, which is at the core of all religions. Gandhi understood that in order to bring about change in the world, one has to first change inside.

Gandhi created a unique concoction which was the result of the extraordinarily powerful combination of spirituality, nationalism, social reforms and self-esteem, all of which are very dear to every individual.

It brings out yet another dimension of leadership: 'By benefiting others we benefit ourselves'. Gandhi probably never planned to create such a concoction to start with, but it happened inadvertently. He started with non-violence and self-righteousness and the rest fell into place one by one. To start with, Gandhi only had very strong spiritual convictions, which paid off in the long run. He gradually became a leader of social reforms with his inclusive approach. He could thus reach out to the poorest of the poor and could motivate not only the ordinary people but also the elitists to commit their lives to truth, non-violence, and service of humanity.

Politicization of Spirituality

Today, the world over, one only needs to witness the politicization of spirituality to be instantly filled with disgust. Politicians cleverly exploit voters on the basis of religion. Within Christianity, for example, it could be Catholic against Protestant. A battle for political power between Shia and Sunni in Islam remains unresolved for the last 1,200 years. Who would ultimately rule the Islamic world is the key question. Leaders like Saddam Hussein, a Sunni, tried to exploit the situation in neighbouring Iran where Shia clergy overthrew the monarchy. Hussein wanted to grab the oil fields near the border and hence weaken Iran's Shia rulers. This failed and led to the bloody Iran–Iraq War of 1980. Saudi Arabia, which is arguably the leader of the world's Sunnis, threw its support to keeping the Sunni minority which is around 30 per cent of the population of Iraq. Even today, Syria, Lebanon and Iraq keep battling each other over the Shia–Sunni issue. In the US, Jewish-Americans who constitute less than 2 per cent of the population do play some role in the country's presidential elections.

In India, vote-bank politics is very prominent, where Muslim votes can be a game-changer for political parties, especially the national ones. Secularism has become the most abused word, used according to convenience and time. Minority vote bank is manipulated along religious as well as caste lines. It appears that leaders of the world in general, and the political masters of India in particular, have probably forgotten what Gandhi taught the world.

Three Dimensions of Human Abilities: IQ, EQ and SQ

We all have three dimensions which could be quantified to some extent: intelligence quotient, the emotional quotient or our spiritual quotient (SQ).

IQ was the first to come up on the scene: it refers to our rational, logical abilities. Leaders during the Industrial Age were highly IQ-driven as they focused more on inventions and production, and had a 'die-hard' business attitude. They possibly looked at a worker as labour, who could or should do a specifically defined work in a specified time. The focus was on higher production and assembly lines. There was little involvement of the emotions. This does not mean that industrialists of that era were heartless; probably, many were great philanthropists. At the same time, emotions had very little role to play in day-to-day work in the industrially dominated era.

The realization of EQ came much later, somewhere by the end of the last century. This became very important as the economy moved from industrial to service-based. The performance of an individual was much more important than the robot-like labour of the Industrial Age. Here, other virtues became more important, including warmth, empathy, managing relationships, self-control and thinking from your heart.

Yet another dimension that played an important part in leadership was the SQ. Earlier it was simply a cutthroat competition where leaders expected you to outperform your peers. In business schools, for example, placements are known to be like a bloodbath: kill or get killed. Just consider the aggression manifested in the very titles of textbooks: *How to Knock Off Your Competition*; or *The Killer's Instinct*. What kind of people are then expected to reach the top? The most self-centred ones? The selfish and the aggressive?

In recent times there has been growing realization that leaders must have their eye on the collective good. And today, leadership is being seen as moving from the heart to the soul. There are leaders at the top who attract good talent and who respect and acknowledge the contribution of their peers towards their success. Such leaders think from their soul.

Benevolent Leadership

This style of leadership creates a high-quality organizational environment where everyone wants to give their best. Such an environment attracts good people who remain loyal to their organization for a very long time. There is growing realization that constantly pushing people to achieve more and yet continue to live in harmony with others, cannot solve society's problems. Therefore, the more important elements of twenty-first-century leadership now include concern for the collective good, collaboration and cooperation.

It is worth noting that Gandhi realized the potency of such an approach as early as the beginning of the twentieth century. Moreover, it is now accepted that a leader who leads from his soul does not require a rank, a formal position or an official mandate in order to become effective. Gandhi, in fact, had proved this point almost a century ago, when, as a nondescript lawyer in South Africa, he managed to obtain the support of his fellow Indians in a country thousands of miles away from home.

If one looks at the governance model of some of the countries of the United Arab Emirates, one sees benevolent leadership in action. Dubai, for instance, is a sheikhdom that has been ruled by the Al Maktoum family since 1833. Sheikhs are the rulers and can keep every penny earned by the state for themselves. In contrast, the sheikhs of Dubai transformed their kingdom from a small town to a vibrant economic hub of the Middle East. Sheikh Rashid, who ruled Dubai from 1958 to 1990, had compassion and a vision of bringing prosperity to his people. He held a 'Majlis' (gathering) every evening to take inputs from the general public and create a forum for debating important issues.

While defining spirituality in the beginning of this chapter I had mentioned that at the core of spirituality lies goodness of the heart and working for the community. By this definition, the sheikhs of Dubai are closer to spirituality than many rich people.

Business Leadership Contexts

William Miller and Debra Miller, in an article argue that business leadership models are rationalist, humanistic, holistic, and spirituality-based. Each of these contexts defines its own business purpose and the ensuing leadership style.

The rational context was the first to emerge during the industrial age of inventions and discoveries at the beginning of the twentieth century. Mass production, assembly lines and the philosophy of doing business was more warlike, with the goal of destroying your competition. The main purpose of business was to create wealth. In other words, it was a dog-eat-dog business scenario. Industry relations laws were created to protect labour and certain protective laws were legislated to protect the consumer.

Gradually the humanistic approach of doing business emerged, where moneymaking was still the prime motive and the emphasis was on collective good and welfare by creating a win-win situation for all stakeholders: the owners, the employees, and the customers. Employees were given a stake in the pie via stock options and bonuses.

Involving employees in management discussions became the norm, which then resulted in employee empowerment. This pushed up productivity as every individual on the shop floor became part-owner in the entire business effort. New concepts emerged, including organization development (OD), team-building and human resources management. Motivation was linked to human needs and clearly bracketed into five levels of hierarchy, conceptualized and popularly known as 'Maslow's hierarchy of needs'.

Next in line was the so-called 'holistic approach' of business leadership, where business was considered to be part of the entire environmental ecosystem. The realization was that if the environment went for a toss, so did the business. Eventually the world moved towards globalization and business focus shifted to benefit all—employees, customers, nature, community, society, and even future generations. Concepts such as CSR (Corporate Social Responsibility) began taking centre-stage.

Customers also preferred to buy products of companies which they believed were ethical and displayed consciousness for the environment. On the leadership and management front, personnel were looked upon as people and new concepts came into practice, like human resource development, learning and development, employee satisfaction, and talent development.

Since the focus was on teamwork, participative engagement and flat organizations (with very little power hierarchy) ensured that every employee was empowered. Along with this came the 360-degree performance appraisals where one superior conducted the appraisal while subordinates gave an objective evaluation of their bosses.

In the beginning of the twenty-first century, the idea of spirituality-based business and leadership emerged. It is still in its infancy but is firmly in place. People in this context started making efforts to bring their spiritual beliefs into their leadership styles. Such beliefs were not necessarily based on any organized religion or faith. These leaders—who had a certain view of spirituality—started leading consciously keeping in mind the spiritual perspective of life as well as the business side.

This was more value-based leadership for the collective good. It aimed at total customer satisfaction, restoring the health of the people, acting responsibly and doing good for society. Wealth creation is not the purpose; rather, wealth was generated in order to sustain this larger purpose. Wealth was like a by-product.

This concept is still evolving as a management principle. For the consumption of a larger audience—comprising those who may not have yet found their spiritual calling—there can be another way of looking at it. Business cannot be for charity (as the two words appear to be mutually exclusive). But even a charitable intent is sufficient. Education, for instance, cannot be free. A good educational institution should charge a fee, but then it must make sure to give much more in return, namely, the best possible education.

Though Mahatma Gandhi was not doing any business or selling material products, he was selling ideas—the idea of fighting for one's rights. Almost a century ago he brought spirituality and dharma into his movement, which soon became political. It was Gandhi who started the spiritualization of politics.

Organizations with Spirituality or 'Do Good' at the Centre of their Leadership Ethos

Non-governmental organizations (NGOs) have charitable intentions for the community in one form or the other. India has more than 3.3 million NGOs, whereas the US has 1.5 million.

Large companies of the Tatas and Birlas have created world-class hospitals, educational and research institutes. The bottomline for such initiatives is to do good for society and, in many cases, for the underprivileged.

Wockhardt, a medical and pharmaceutical company with an annual turnover of around Rs 1,000 crore, is a company driven by ethics, which believes in the joy of performing. The organization's top leadership believes that 'Joy is not in things but is within us.' Their Vision Statement is thus: 'To strive with excellence to fulfill the needs of the community in its chosen field of medical treatment.'

Hard Rock Café was co-founded by Issac Tigrett and the

first outlet opened in London in 1971. The idea was to create a cosy place where people from all walks of life could come and enjoy rock music and American cuisine.

Tigrett, along with his partner, observed that in London those days, social classes still existed; in fact they were completely separated. There was hardly any place where a baker and a banker could meet and eat. Tigrett and his partner were then motivated to create a restaurant which they envisioned as an alternative: a 'classless' one. It was a hit from day one. The clients ranged from politicians to plumbers, bankers to labourers. Tigrett's values for inclusive approach were heightened to spiritual levels when he traelled to India and was influenced by Satya Sai Baba. He learnt and appreciated the mantra 'Love all, serve all'. He assimilated the meaning of selfless and unconditional love. He not only created a unique place for his customers but also for his employees, which was like a family for all. People who came from broken homes and joined the Hard Rock Café family got love, respect and affection. It became a second home for them. This created much loyalty and integrity amongst the staff. Tigrett started spreading his message of love by putting 'Love all, serve all,' on menus, caps, t-shirts, bills and kitchens.

The business soon expanded worldwide, and today its net worth is in excess of $500 million. In Tigrett's words, 'All I did was to put spirit and business together and to that bowl I added love. I didn't care about anything but people. Just cherish them, be sensitive to them and look after them.'

We follow something similar at our college, MILE (Management Institute for Leadership and Excellence). We have a fully student-run institute. Student committees take charge of almost all the day-to-day affairs. Events, administration, the cafeteria are all managed by the students. The library is handled by a library committee. We have a unique open library where books are kept on open racks and not in lockers. There is no policing and we don't have a librarian! This experiment has been a runaway success and has worked very well without the loss of even one book in the last five years. This is spirituality in practice and it works.

The rationalistic context is now on the decline, the humanistic in its prime, the holistic is developing and the spiritual is emerging.

If one looks at spirituality more holistically, it would appear that it has great many applications. It finds its application in business, entertainment, politics as well as education.

Mahatma Gandhi saw politics as an extension of spirituality and motivated people to create a historic national movement as early as the first quarter of the twentieth century.

'The contemporary form of true greatness lies in a civilization founded on the spirituality of work.'
—Simone Weil, French philosopher and political activist

LEADERSHIP LESSONS FROM A SAINT WITHOUT AUTHORITY

- A leader, in the context of modern management, must lead from his soul.
- Though the idea of spirituality-based leadership and business emerged only in the twenty-first century, Mahatma Gandhi had lived this almost a hundred years ago.
- Today there is a growing realization and acceptance of value-based leadership for the collective good, wherein a leader takes care of the entire ecosystem.
- Organizations with 'do good' as part of their vision-mission ultimately do better than those who look only for profits through a highly narrow outlook.

12

SIMPLIFY YOUR LIFE

Minimalistic Living

'If your reputation sucks, none of it matters. People with lousy products, crummy business practices, and shady backgrounds get found out. And word spreads with frightening speed.'

—Sonia Simone, writer and marketer

Gandhi's Most Important Message for Business Leaders and Gen Next

Corporate leaders, businessmen and the current generation seem to be confused about just how much is too much. They are not sure what will make them happy. There is a constant struggle to find answers, look for quick-fix solutions or chase some spiritual gurus to find solace, peace of mind and some comfort—whatever the price. Indeed, the catch word is 'price'! One wants to pay for peace of mind and then hope to get it too.

The solution to the problem lies in the statement itself. People feel that with the power of money, you can buy everything. If you can buy a mansion, a yacht, some fancy cars, designer clothes, trendy electronic gadgets, then why can't you buy peace and contentment, too?

Today this problem has become even more relevant because of two reasons: first, that too much is available in the materialistic space; and second, in the race to acquire all that is available, we have accelerated our pace and complicated our lives.

Brand Bombardment

We are exposed every day to advertisements through TV, radio, print, movies, hoardings, the internet, and even mobile phones. Though the figures given by different studies vary, it is said that each one of us is exposed to roughly 1,500 to 3,000 advertisements every single day. That would amount to half a million to one million a year. We may absorb some of them and our brain may reject most, but at the end of the day they do leave an impression on our minds. Ads make us crave for products; they are designed to lure us into buying the stuff we may not even need.

The human mind is highly impressionable and unfortunately, these advertisements manage to create certain brand images in our minds. In the last two decades the younger population has been made very brand-conscious by these advertising campaigns. So much so that we have started linking our self-esteem to the product price tags. Think of it, you are more important than the clothes you wear! If a three-piece branded suit costing Rs. 20,000 makes or breaks your self-esteem, then your total worth is only Rs. 20,000! If you have substance, you need not hide behind expensive clothes.

Too Many Choices

Our lives are made more difficult because of too many choices made available to us every day—holiday packages, cars, mobile phones, jackets, suits, TVs, footwear, food, cameras, bikes, home loans, insurance policies, laptops, furniture: all of them offer us multiple options. Different features, differential price points and a variety of payment options for each of these could make it very difficult for a buyer to make a decision.

In his book, *Paradox of Choices*, psychologist Barry Schwarts argues that while more choices give us freedom to choose what we want, this also makes us unhappy. The unhappiness in an affluent society stems from the fact that so many choices raise expectations. And even if you initially think that you have made a terrific choice, you may still end up feeling that you could have possibly got something even better.

Schwarts says that in the US, for example, the spread of products in a reasonably large grocery store could be mindboggling: some 285 varieties of cookies, seventy-five kinds of iced tea, 230 soups, 175 salad dressings, forty toothpastes, 135 shampoos. He says that the kind of electronic hardware which is available today allows you to configure your stereo systems in 6.5 million different ways!

Once Schwarts went to the store to buy himself a simple pair of jeans. The sales staff asked him, 'Which one are you looking for? Stone-washed, acid-washed, hard-washed, or easy fit, slim fit, relax fit, casual fit, loose fit or butterfly, zipper fly or single ply, double ply or cut pockets, straight pockets?'

He replied, 'I need the kind of jeans that I have been wearing all these years.' The sales staff said, 'But we don't have that kind.'

So can affluence buy happiness?

Gandhi's Frugal Lifestyle

Gandhi earned the title of 'Mahatma' primarily because of his simple lifestyle. He was exposed to an affluent way of life at the young age of eighteen when he went to England to study law. He was impressed by the dressing sense of the British and tried to emulate them in letter and spirit. He wore expensive suits, fancy hats and stylish footwear while he lived in England. During his initial days in South Africa he also wanted to impress people by donning British attire. He gradually realized that no matter what he wore, the whites in South Africa still looked down upon him, as they looked down upon all Indians. He also realized that deeds and actions would create a more lasting impact rather than fancy attire, which was superficial.

Influenced by the Gita, Gandhi wanted to purify his life by the concept of non-possession and equality for all. In both his ashrams in South Africa he built a culture of community living, labour by all, and a very simple lifestyle with self-reliance at its core. He found peace and tranquility in frugal living.

He brought about a revolution in the idea of simple living and high thinking with his charkha, with which he spun cloth to make his own clothes. Khadi thus became his trademark (and has remained so). It is not that Gandhi was not exposed to the material goods available in his time; he took a conscious decision to shun them and lead a simple life.

When he visited people in the South as he was touring India, he realized that most did not have enough clothes to cover themselves. This prompted him to start wearing a loincloth, which covered barely half of his body. In all he had about ten worldly possessions—his loincloth, sandals, spectacles, walking stick, plate, bowl, pocket watch, a chaddar, a shawl and a prayer book.

His routine was simple and followed the principle of 'finding joy in small things'. He would personally tend to the animals, bask in the sun and massage himself with oil. Perhaps the most startling lesson one can derive from Gandhi's lifestyle is that you don't have to be dressed in the most expensive clothes and flaunt your wealth and power by possessing all that is available to be famous or to be noticed by the world. It is your deeds and sense of purpose that speak best for you.

If you want to put this into practise then learn to shed your possessions gradually. If you have, say, one hundred things for personal use, see how many you can do without. You will be surprised to identify a number of things that you do not require. Drop ten things at a time and bring the number down to fifty. This will remove a huge part of the stress from your life.

Simplistic living became a major part of the Gandhian way of life which many people influenced by Gandhi adopted and still do. He summed up his philosophy by saying: 'The world has enough for everyone's need, but not enough for everyone's greed.' This becomes all the more relevant today when the gap between the haves and the have-nots has become very huge. There are people who have half a dozen houses and an equal number of cars. They have huge bank balances and much more than what they can actually eat. On the other hand, out of 7.1 billion people in the world, around 870 million live in poverty. This means that one out of every eight human beings on this planet is malnourished.

Leaders must motivate their teams towards simple living and helping the poor. Learn the joy of giving; we have so many things inside our own homes that we never use. It could be books, clothes or utensils or other things we could do without.

Learn to conserve. Use the stairs instead of a lift; use a

bicycle instead of a car. Use a two-wheeler for short trips and don't feel small. One could grow some vegetables in the backyard. Make home-made wine, lemonade, ginger ale, jams, and bread. And most importantly, don't waste food, or other resources like water and electricity.

Just How Much Do We Need?

While going for route marches and out-bounds, armed forces personnel have to remain in the jungles or hilly terrain for days at a stretch. They follow the concept of 'living off the land', being self-contained and having zero dependency on the outside world.

Each one has to carry his own stuff, besides weapons and ammunition. You can stuff your backpack with whatever you want, but you have to carry it yourself and as you walk tens of miles every day every gram of weight matters. That is the time you realize that you can do without many things. You are carrying your clothes, your sleeping kit, blankets, your toiletries, your mess tins, water bottles, torch, first-aid kit and rations for a week! All on your back.

That is the time you use your better judgement and carry only that which is 'most essential'. Mind you, one still manages to do pretty well with so little for days together.

Comforts and needs are a state of mind. We amass so much but hardly use a fraction of what we have during our entire life. How we unnecessarily accumulate objects came to my mind when we were shifting home. The movers and packers took a full day to pack up our clothes and all the household goods. They required more than a hundred large cartons. As this was being done, I noticed our dog Fluffy wagging her tail as she sat on her little rug. I looked at her, and I realized that all she needed to live comfortably was a couple of bowls for water and milk, one collar, a leash, a rug, a tiny blanket and one warm jacket for winters! Fluffy, I thought, lived the life of a saint.

Power to Say 'No'

Truly one of the biggest virtues of great men and women is the power of self-denial. If you have the ability to say no to the good things then you are able to keep your temptations in check. Once this happens you will be able to say no to a bribe, no to flattery (which is also a bribe), no to a gift, no to a free ride. No to anything that is tempting.

Gandhi's frugal eating habits, his simple attire and absolute essential possessions reflected his strong character. He developed strong willpower by saying no to food and protesting by fasting.

Enjoy the Moment: Get Involved

In the good old days, people went for picnics and hikes with only their bare essentials. Getting together and travelling in a group itself was fun. One didn't carry complicated paraphernalia. Instead one carried raw foods and cooked it under difficult conditions. Getting involved and participation was the biggest satisfaction for everyone.

Today we miss out on all that. The younger generation spends more time sitting in front of laptops or tablets, or on their mobile phones, or strolling in the malls. You chat, yes, but that too on mobile phones, iPads or computers. Progress is in fact disconnecting people, instead of connecting them as is being claimed. Video games are making children physically weak and inactive.

Just take note of how much you speak on your phone. If you are a little conscious and cautious, you can save a good amount of time in a day for more productive work. Indians alone speak for 500 billion minutes in a month, which amounts to six trillion minutes per year! In terms of cost it comes to a whopping Rs 200,000 crore, which we all collectively bear.

Products are fully loaded, to be sure, but do we use all their features? Look at your cell phone, with all its applications. You may be using only a fraction of them.

Therefore, simplify your life. Make your life clean, lean and mean.

Mahatmas of the World

It is intriguing that people go to saints and fakirs to seek peace and prosperity. These saints and fakirs have no worldly possessions to offer to their devotees, simply because they own none. Sai Baba of Shirdi, Khwaja Moinuddin Chishti of Ajmer, Gautam Buddha, or even Mahavir—they all shunned materialistic possessions. Look at the founders of any religion or faith, they all preach to shun materialistic possessions. The Dalai Lama still does so.

Mahatma Gandhi learnt from these sages across the ages. He heeded their lessons that helped him lead a life of simplicity. He preached through practice: that was his biggest strength. It was the lifestyle he led that motivated people to follow him. How could anyone oppose a person who lives so humbly? He was spotlessly honest and therefore no one could dare raise a finger at him. That is why Rabindranath Tagore gave him the title of Mahatma and the nation called him 'Bapu' or father.

Today people are leaving high-paying jobs to join NGOs at

just a fraction of their previous salaries. They do this to simplify their lives, stay away from the so-called 'rat race' and engage in something more meaningful. You need not become a monk, but you can drastically simplify your life by taking a conscious decision.

Down-to-earth, Rich and Famous

Once, as I was taking my suitcase out of the car to catch my flight at the Pune airport, I noticed a familiar face pushing a luggage trolley. On a closer examination I realized that it was Ratan Tata in a pinstriped suit, slowly moving forward in a queue of passengers. No fanfare, no send-offs, no chamchas; not even an escort! Immediately my respect for the man notched up a hundred times. It is funny when you find a send-off party of more than fifty men and women all having garlands and bouquets in their hands at the airport to see off some neta or VVIP. Ratan Tata, chairman emeritus of such a formidable group of companies such as his, many times drives his own car, takes his dogs for a walk and even runs his own errands himself.

Narayana Murthy is another fine example. Even after becoming a billionaire with a net worth of $1.55 billion, the non-executive chairman of Infosys draws a salary of one rupee per year! He likes a simple lifestyle and still stays in a small house.

Then there is Dr A.P.J. Abdul Kalam, India's former president. Dr Kalam was born to a boat owner in Tamil Nadu and worked as a newspaper vendor to support his studies. He went on to become a scientist of repute. Even then he kept to his simple lifestyle, with his worldly possessions not filling up more than two trunks, one for clothes and one for his books. He rose to the country's presidency and yet remained humble. Once, as he was travelling in America, he was subjected by airport personnel to the usual security measures, including frisking. The former Indian president did not make any fuss and cooperated, even as he was well within his rights to lodge a protest with the government. Such is the greatness of this man. Most of us are nothing compared to him and yet our demands are loud and high as are our tantrums.

Warren Buffet was declared the richest man in the world in 2008, yet he still lives in a house which he bought in 1958 for $31,500, and lives a simple life. He is one of the world's greatest philanthropists, giving 99 per cent of his wealth to charity. He does not use a cell phone, has no computer on his desk and enjoys playing bridge almost twelve hours a week.

If such successful people can live a simple life, there is no reason why others—who are ordinary compared to them—cannot let go of certain things and make their lives less stressful and comfortable. All these examples demonstrate that comfort and peace lies in simplicity and not complexity.

'Fools ignore complexity. Pragmatists suffer it. Some can avoid it. Geniuses remove it.'
—Alan Perlis, American computer scientist

LEADERSHIP LESSONS FROM A SAINT WITHOUT AUTHORITY

- To have peace of mind is cheaper than we think. In fact, one does not have to spend in order to lead a stress-free life.
- Just making our life simpler is enough to relieve ourselves of stress.
- We should look at branding and advertising as a way of intoxicating our minds. Look at them as information alone and don't get lured into buying whatever is being advertised.
- Today too many choices are made available to us as consumers. Make a conscious effort not to get entangled in this 'multiple option syndromes'.
- We don't have to live like hermits, but we can and should gradually cut down our possessions and requirements. It gives a tremendous feeling of liberation.
- Remember, the price tag of your shirt is not *your* price tag. Never link the two. You are too precious and priceless compared to what your wear.
- Constantly remind yourself that you have enough. Do not fill up your home with stuff that you do not need.
- Enjoy the moment, find joy in simple things. Simplify your life.